A PHOTOGRAPHIC GUIDE TO

BIRDS

OF

INDIA AND
NEPAL

BIKRAM GREWAL

D0528722

Reprinted in 2010
This edition published in 2007
First published in the UK in 1995
New Holland Publishers (UK) Ltd
London • Cape Town • Sydney • Auckland

Garfield House, 86-88 Edgware Road, London W2 2EA, United Kingdom
80 McKenzie Street, Cape Town 8001, South Africa
Unit 1, 66 Gibbes Street, Chatswood, NSW 2067, Australia
218 Lake Road, Northcote, Auckland, New Zealand

10 9 8 7 6

ISBN 978 1 84537 982 7

Cartography by Gulmohur Press, New Delhi, India

Reproduction by P & W Graphics Pte Ltd, Singapore
Printed and bound in Malaysia by Times Offset (M) Sdn Bhd

Front cover photograph: Painted Stork (Khalid Ghani/NHPA)
Title page photograph: Scarlet Minivet (Krupakar Senani)

Acknowledgements
The author would like to thank Sumit Sen Bittu Sahgal, Nikhil Devasar,
Clement Francis and Rajat Desai for being friends. Alpana Khare for my
greatest companion in life and our children Nikhat, Keya, Raghu and
Samiha for being there.

Contents

Introduction

Birds have always fascinated human beings; birdwatching provides a practical, and indeed challenging outlet for this fascination. Most birds are widely distributed, being found in many states and countries unless restricted by specialization to a specific habitat or, more importantly in the present context, by man's threat to and destruction of habitat.

Ornithologists group birds into genera and families of closely related species. If one learns to recognize birds by the characteristics of their families, it simplifies the identification of any new birds that one encounters. The ability to identify birds, therefore, is largely a matter of familiarity gained through experience and by concentrating on the differences and similarities between the various birds. The ability to distinguish different birds and their calls is simply a matter of repeated contact and careful observation, combined with the enthusiast's own experience and expertise.

The Indian Subcontinent, comprising India, Nepal, Bhutan, Bangladesh, Pakistan and Sri Lanka, is richly endowed with bird life, with no fewer than 1200 species of birds belonging to some 400 different genera and spread over nearly 80 families – a veritable eldorado for those interested in birds and birdwatching. Incorporating the world's largest population of vegetarians and non-hunters, many parts of the region provide safe shelter for the birds and they in return act as though they adore being admired; precisely the relationship that this book seeks to foster. Its pages informatively describe and illustrate over 250 species of the more common, novel and photogenic birds of the Indian Subcontinent. The birds of the Himalayas and the Western Ghats, regions especially rich in their biodiversity, are well represented, as are those of the plains and plateaux of India.

Because the Subcontinent lies in the Tropics, there are those who believe that it has at most two seasons, the 'cool-hot' and 'hot-hot'. What they forget, however, is that the Tropics include only peninsular India, and that the entire northern region stretching to the Himalayas lies north of the Tropic of Cancer. The climatic and vegetational range is thus virtually limitless, from blistering cold alpine snowlines to dark, steamy, tropical rainforests and soaring, arid deserts. The monsoons bring rain in regular cycles, transforming the dry landscape into a lush green, which the sun then turns into a dry brown, and so the cycle continues. From the grasslands of the bustards, to the shaded, forested valleys of the whistling thrushes, the Subcontinent provides a variety of habitats that few regions can surpass, and a landscape that keeps pace with the seasons.

Besides the diversity of its resident bird life, the Subcontinent is also host to a number of foreign ambassadors, the palearctic migrants seeking refuge from the northern winter. These birds begin arriving and spreading into the region between August and October and depart between March and May. For those that breed just across the borders, it is just a hop, albeit a high one, over the Himalayas, but for those that don't, it could be a very long, jet-lagged flight from within the Arctic Circle.

The number of species that a bird enthusiast is able to see depends very largely on the number of habitats and zones that he or she is able to visit. The Indian Subcontinent boasts some 15 different bioclimatic zones and vegetational regions. The variety that is created out of the natural zones and the man-made or man-altered habitats is vast. Combinations of various habitats form mosaics, which harbour their own unique mix of species, adding an extra dimension and charm to the pleasures of birdwatching in the Subcontinent.

Most of this book is devoted to bird identification, each species given a representative photograph accompanied by a description to assist in the process of recognition. There are, in addition, a section on bird structure, a glossary defining ornithological terms, and a section providing information on the identification of birds and the more practical aspects of birdwatching in the field. A selection of suggested reading and useful addresses is included at the end.

How to use this book

The species included in the guide are arranged according to the widely accepted species numbering system provided by S. Dillon Ripley in his *A Synopsis of the Birds of India and Pakistan*. The species number appears in the top right-hand corner of the description and enables the reader to cross-check information about the bird with that in the comprehensive *Handbook of the Birds of India and Pakistan, Together with those of Bangladesh, Nepal, Bhutan and Sri Lanka* by Salim Ali and S. Dillon Ripley.

The photographs
Each species included in the book is accompanied by one colour photograph. In many species, the males and females are identical and so identification from the photograph will present no problems. In the case of some species, however, males and females have different plumages, and in a few these can even vary with the time of year. In such cases we have depicted the male.

The species descriptions
The descriptions provide detailed information about each species included in the guide, as follows:

Common name – in all cases, the most popular and widely accepted vernacular or English name in this region is used. There is at the present time, however, considerable confusion in this matter, different authors using different sets of names.

Scientific name – each species has a unique scientific name recognized the world over in any language.

Length – this is the distance between the tip of the bill and the tip of the tail.

Appearance – in the text, reference is made to features and plumage details appropriate to the species in question.

Flight – because birds are often seen in flight, this is an important feature in their description. Where relevant, reference is made to the size and shape of the wings, colours and patterns.

Behaviour – each species of bird has behaviour patterns unique to its kind. These govern aspects of day-to-day life such as feeding, courtship, response to predators and whether the bird is solitary or gregarious.

Habitat – generally speaking, birds are faithful to a particular habitat which caters to all their daily needs of food, shelter and protection.

Voice – voice can be extremely important in identification. Among the passerines – the so-called 'perching birds' or 'song birds' – diagnostic songs are often delivered at the start of the breeding season. A much wider variety of birds, including the passerines, have distinctive calls, and experienced birdwatchers are able to identify a large proportion of common birds by sound alone.

Abundance – all the birds in this guide are common at least somewhere within the Indian Subcontinent.

Maps – providing concise and easily accessible information about the range of each species.

Corner tabs – these provide an at-a-glance reference relating to the species family groups. See key opposite.

Glossary

Axillaries Underwing feathers at the base of the wing, forming the so-called 'armpits'.
Commensal Living together with man for mutual benefit.
Coverts Feathers on the upper and lower surfaces of the wing that assist streamlining in flight.
Eye-stripe Tract of feathers that runs through the eye.
Flight feathers Feathers used for flight; the outer primaries and the inner secondaries of the wings.
Irruption Mass movement of a population from one area to

Key to corner tabs

 Grebes & cormorants

 Pelicans, herons, storks & cranes, ibises & flamingoes

 Swans, geese & ducks

 Raptors

 Gamebirds

 Rails & crakes

 Waders

 Skuas, gulls & terns

 Pigeons, doves & sandgrouse

 Parrots

 Cuckoos & relatives

 Owls

 Nightjars

 Kingfishers, bee-eaters & hoopoes

 Hornbills

 Barbets

 Woodpeckers

 Larks

 Swallows & martins

 Shrikes

 Orioles

 Drongos

 Starlings & mynas

 Crows

 Wood shrikes & minivets

 Leafbirds & relatives

 Bulbuls

 Babblers & relatives

 Flycatchers & relatives

 Warblers, prinias & tailor birds

 Thrushes & relatives

 Tits & nuthatches

 Wagtails

 Sunbirds & relatives

 Sparrows, munias, finches & buntings

another, usually in response to exhaustion of the food supply.

Juvenile A young bird in its first full plumage.

Mantle The feathers on the back.

Migration The movement by some species from one area to another, the two regions being well defined and their occurrence predictable.

Moult The shedding and replacement of worn and damaged feathers at regular intervals.

Passage migrant A migrant bird that is seen when it stops off to rest and feed during migration from its breeding grounds to its wintering quarters.

Passerine An extensive group of birds, also known as the 'perching birds' because of this ability.

Plumes Long, showy feathers often acquired at the start of the breeding season and used for display.

Race Populations of the same species that are isolated geographically so that they seldom encounter one another and have subtle difference in plumage and behaviour.

Raptor A term applied to diurnal birds of prey.

Resident Present within an area throughout the year.

Species Individuals belong to the same species if they are capable of breeding and producing viable offspring.

Speculum Shiny area of feathering on the secondary feathers of the wings of many ducks.

Summer plumage The plumage acquired at the start of the breeding season.

Supercilium The tract of feathers that runs above the eye and eye-stripe as a discrete stripe.

Wader A category of birds often with long legs and bills, including sandpipers, plovers and curlews.

Wildfowl The family of birds comprising swans, geese and ducks.

Wingspan The length from one wingtip to the other when fully extended in flight.

Winter plumage The plumage seen during the non-breeding winter months.

Bird structure and appearance

The different species of birds vary greatly both in terms of size and shape. Despite the apparent dissimilarity between say a tit and a white stork, both these species, and all others, have many features in common. The basic plan of the skeleton will be essentially the same; even the layout of the plumage will be similar, the feathers growing in tracts which all birds have in common.

A bird's feathers serve a variety of functions. The most obvious of these have to do with flight. The primaries and secondaries on the wings provide much of the power needed for flight while the coverts on the wings and the contour feathers on the body aid streamlining and an aerodynamic shape.

Feathers also serve to provide the insulation needed to maintain the bird's body temperature and are assisted in this by the underlying down feathers on the body. Lastly, the feathers are often coloured, the patterns produced providing camouflage in some species and colourful display in others.

The illustration shows a stylized line drawing of a typical bunting. The feathered areas of the head can be clearly seen as can the feather tracts of the wings when held at rest. In this posture, inevitably, some of the wing feathers are partially concealed. The relative lengths of the different feathers and the presence or absence of features such as wing-bars on particular tracts of feathers can be important in identification.

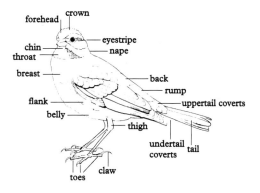

Study the illustration and try to memorize the names and locations of the most important parts of the bird's body. Feather tracts are often represented by discrete blocks of colour which can vary from species to species or according to seasonal plumage. A knowledge of this feathering will enable you to make direct comparisons between species and refer more easily to the descriptions in the text.

Identifying birds

Identifying birds can sometimes be a rather frustrating experience, especially for the beginner. When seen by seasoned observers and under ideal conditions, most of the birds in this book should be readily identifiable; birdwatchers new to the pastime may have difficulty under some circumstances. Reassuringly, your ability will without doubt improve over the years and you should be comforted by the knowledge that, however experienced the birdwatcher, there will always be some sightings that defy identification.

Your birdwatching skills will improve with time and experience. Here are some of the important aspects of bird life and birdwatching on which to concentrate.

Size

Measuring the length of a bird in the field is clearly not an option in most cases and so the birdwatcher must learn to gauge size. This is not always as easy as it sounds since optical aids – binoculars and telescopes – can often distort the apparent size. Try to compare the bird in question with a nearby individual of known species or an object of known size, remembering to make allowances for foreshortening in perspective if the two are not in the same plane of focus.

Shape

Birds of particular family groups often share distinctive shapes. For example, herons and egrets are, by and large, long-legged and long-necked birds while plovers have short, stubby bills, dumpy bodies and longish legs.

The overall shape of the body and the relative sizes of the head, bill and legs are obviously important. The bird's stance and posture should, however, also be noted. Some birds perch and sit upright while others adopt a more horizontal posture; non-perching birds also have a range of postures and stances, and it should not be forgotten that these can vary according to the behaviour of the bird.

Colour

When identifying a new bird, make careful observations of the patterns and colours of the plumage. Lighting can be crucial in the observation of colour so take this into account.

It should also be borne in mind that a bird's plumage can vary according to the time of the year and the sex of the individual, so you need to establish whether you are looking at a bird in breeding plumage or a non-breeding bird in winter plumage. Juveniles, which often have cleaner-looking feathering in the autumn than adults, are invariably different in appearance from their parents.

Behaviour

The behaviour of a bird can give vital clues to its identification, although a degree of patient observation may be needed to discern the more important patterns. Watch, for example, the way in which the bird feeds, whether on the ground or among foliage, or its flight pattern and response to others of the same or different species.

Habitat

Each species is perfectly adapted to feed in a characteristic way in a particular habitat, and only under exceptional circumstances will it be found elsewhere. There are, of course, species which are exceptions to the rule. With most bird species, a knowledge of their habitat preferences can greatly improve the chances of being able to find them.

Voice

When it comes to a knowledge of bird songs and calls, there is no substitute for field experience. Most birdwatchers will in time learn about all the more common and widespread species. This can be a very satisfying and, at the very least, provides you with a basis for comparison when dealing with unfamiliar calls.

Jizz

The 'jizz' of a bird is a combination of all the features and aspects discussed above and others, seen through eyes of an experienced birdwatcher. Given years of observation, some people can identify birds even in poor light and at a considerable range. Clues used might be the flight pattern of a speck on the horizon or the feeding pattern of a distant wader far out on the mud flat. At least part of the skill, however, derives from having the background knowledge to make a 'best guess' at the most likely species in a particular habitat at a certain time of year.

Going birdwatching

Having familiarized yourself with the layout of the guide, it is now time to go birdwatching. Although at the simplest level, all you need is a pair of eyes, some expenditure on equipment can greatly increase the pleasure derived from the pursuit. Also, the development of fieldcraft skills and a knowledge of when, where and how to watch birds can enhance the experience.

Equipment

A pair of binoculars is part of the uniform of every birdwatcher (along with waterproof boots and clothing). It goes without saying that the more you spend, the better the quality of the binoculars. There are numerous models on the market with price tags that range from under £50 to nearly £1,000. However, you do not necessarily have to spend a fortune to acquire a good pair so visit a reputable dealer and try out a few before you make a purchase.

You will find that all binoculars bear a set of numbers which provide clues of their likely value to the birdwatcher. A typical pair might have the numbers 8×40 on the casing. The first number indicates the degree of magnification of the lenses and the second is a measure of their light-gathering capacity and hence the brightness of the image. Do not be tempted into purchasing anything with a magnification greater than 10 or less than 6. The second number should not be less than 30 or the image will be too dark, nor perhaps more than 50 since the binoculars may be too heavy to hold still.

The best advice when buying a pair of binoculars would perhaps be to purchase the ones you feel most comfortable with. The same goes for telescopes which nowadays also come in all shapes and sizes. With a telescope you also need a tripod to stand it on for prolonged observation: the dedicated

birdwatcher soon becomes laden with all manner of
paraphernalia!

When and where to go birdwatching

Time of day, time of year and weather all have an important
bearing on the variety and numbers of birds in a given
habitat. Before planning an outing that involves any travel, it
is often wise to sit and consider your options.

Habitats offer differing birdwatching opportunities throughout the year. Woodlands, for example, are often at their best
in the spring when territorial birds are in full song and the
leaves are not fully open. Although birdwatching is good
throughout the morning, arrive as early as you can after dawn
for the best chorus. Woodlands in summer are often rather
uninspiring for the birdwatcher but, perhaps surprisingly,
winter has much to recommend it. Mixed flocks of small birds
roam the trees and the lack of leaves makes observation easy.

While many common species are spread over large areas,
others are limited not just to a region but also to habitat.
Some birds of the conifer forests of the hills, for example, will
only be found there. City gardens are homes for many
species, including tailorbirds, sunbirds, white-eyes, babblers
and mynas. Shallow lagoons, inland jheels or shallow lakes
and rivers are rich habitats for water birds like pelicans,
storks, cranes and egrets.

Sooner or later, birdwatchers are lured to the coast. Many
birds of the coast are distinctive. Typical is the Indian Reef
heron. Again, different areas of coast are best at different
times of year. Seabird cliffs and other nesting areas are best in
spring and summer, while estuaries come into their own in
autumn and winter.

A large number of waterfowls migrate each winter to India
from central and northern Asia. The Siberian Crane is one such
bird which comes to the Keoladeo Ghana National Park at
Bharatpur in Rajasthan every winter. Summer visitors are
much fewer. The multicoloured Indian Pitta is one such bird.
It winters in south India and Sri Lanka, and visits the
deciduous forest and the scrubland of the Himalayan foothills
and the north-west around May, staying until it has bred.

Further reading

Ali, S. and Ripley S.D (1987) *The Compact Handbook of the
Birds of India and Pakistan*. Bombay: Oxford University Press

Grewal, B. (1998) *A Photographic Guide to the Birds of the
Himalayas*. London: New Holland.

Grewal, B, Harvey, B. and Pfister,O. (2002) *A photographic
Guide to the Birds of India*. Singapore: Periplus Editions.

Grimmet, R Inskipp, T. & Inskipp, C. (1998) *Birds of the Indian Subcontinent*. UK: A&C Black.

Kazmierczak, K. & van Perlo, B. (2000) *A Field Guide to the Birds of the Indian Subcontinent*. UK: Pica Press

Useful addresses

Bombay Natural History Society
Hornbill House
Shahid Bhagat Singh Marg
Bombay-400023

World Wide Fund for Nature India
172B, Lodi Estate
New Delhi-110003

Bird Conservation Nepal
P.O. Box 536
Kathmandu
Nepal

Delhi Bird Club
www.Delhibird.net

Bengal Birds
www.Kolkatabirds.com

Oriental Bird Club
www.orientalbirdclub.com

Great Crested Grebe *Podiceps cristatus* 50cm   3

Joanna Van Gruisen

The largest grebe in the Indian region and much larger than the Little Grebe. As with other grebes almost tailless, with the legs placed far back. Overall dark greyish-brown above and whitish below, with a long, slender, white neck. Two backwardly directed ear tufts, smaller in the female and largely absent in winter. White on wing prominent in flight. Found scattered on reed-bordered or vegetation-covered fresh and littoral waters. Dives without a splash and when alarmed has a habit of swimming underwater, surfacing, taking a look and repeating the process till sufficient distance has been gained.

Little Grebe *Podiceps ruficollis* 23cm   5

Joanna Van Gruisen

Now swimming on the surface of the water and down under the very next moment, the Little Grebe is more loath to fly than to dive. Dark brown above with chestnut on the sides of the neck. Whitish below with some white in the wing, the latter visible in flight. Glossier and richer colours when breeding. Young striped and spotted. Produces a shrill, tittering trill when playing about in the evenings, chasing others about on the water. Exclusively aquatic, being found in ponds, irrigation tanks and reservoirs. Catches fish, tadpoles, and the like, underwater. Widespread all over the Indian region.

Great White Pelican *Pelecanus onocrotalus* 183cm 20

A huge white bird with some black on the wings and an overall rosy tinge. Forehead feathers form a pointed projection over the bill unlike those of the Grey Pelican. Sexes alike, but female smaller. Young pale brown on the upperparts, white below. Bill blue with the bare skin of pouch and face yellow, brighter when breeding. Short stout legs and feet pink with the webs being yellow. On larger bodies of water of North India, sometimes aggregating in large numbers. Groups feed by herding shoals of fish and scooping them up in their large bill pouches. Much given to soaring on thermals.

Grey Pelican *Pelecanus philippensis* 152cm 21

Slightly smaller than the Great White Pelican, this species is greyish overall with no black in the wings. Short, stout legs, large webbed feet and the bill is flesh-coloured with blue spots on upper mandible. Pouch is dull purple with darkish markings. Feet dark brown. Sexes alike. Young pale brown above and white below. Purely aquatic; solitary as well as in large gatherings. It is a resident species but subject to local movements. Is more widespread in the non-breeding season. Breeds colonially on trees locally in southern and north-eastern India, and Sri Lanka. Shares general habits with other pelicans.

Great Cormorant *Phalacrocorax carbo* 80cm　　　26

S Nagaraj

Largest of the region's cormorants, this bird is bigger than a Pariah Kite. Overall black with a metallic sheen, white facial skin and throat, and white thigh patches. Bright yellow gular pouch and silky white plumes on head and neck. In the non-breeding season, no white thigh patches and the gular pouch less bright. Sexes alike. Young are dull brown above and white below. Less gregarious and less common than the other cormorants. Usually found individually or in small groups. Frequents large bodies of water, both fresh and salty. Shares the typical cormorant habit of perching upright on branch or rock with wings and tail spread out, drying itself after a swim.

Indian Cormorant *Phalacrocorax fuscicollis* 63cm　　　27

Krupakar Senani

The only other large cormorant of the region, in-between the Little and the Large Cormorant in size, but still larger than a Pariah Kite. Overall bronze-black, glossy when breeding. Sexes alike. A white tuft on side of head when breeding, and yellowish gular pouch when not breeding, distinguishes it from the Little Cormorant. Young are scaly bronze-brown above and white below with the flanks mottled. Found in both fresh and salty waters. Gregarious. As with other cormorants, has feathers which get wet, and have to be dried after a swim. Colonial nesting, subject to local movements.

Little Cormorant *Phalacrocorax niger* 51cm 28

The smallest and most common of the region's cormorants, this species is just larger than a Jungle Crow. Overall black with a coloured sheen, the breeding and non-breeding plumages differ slightly. The short crest and whitish feathers on the head absent in the non-breeding season. The all-black gular skin and throat when not breeding and the small white throat patch when breeding distinguishes it from the Indian Cormorant. Young brown with paler underparts, but with white throat and centre of abdomen. Gregarious and colonial nesting. Shares general habits with other cormorants.

Otto Pfister

Darter *Anhinga rufa* 90cm 29

Joanna Van Gruisen

Though related to the cormorants, the Darter is quite distinctive from them. A large size, larger than the Pariah Kite, long snake-like neck, and a dagger-like beak characteristic. Black above, streaked and mottled with silvery-grey on back and wings. Brown head and neck with a white stripe down side of upper neck. Swims with just the snake-like head above the water, body completely submerged. Like the cormorants, needs to dry its feathers after a swim, the wettable feathers enabling it to dive easily. Sometimes given to soaring on thermals. Essentially a freshwater species.

Grey Heron *Ardea cinerea* 98cm

Joanna Van Gruisen

A large, striking-looking heron, ashy-grey above and greyish-white below. Long orange-yellow, sometimes pinkish, legs when breeding; non-breeding greenish-brown. Large yellow beak, and a dotted band along the centre of fore-neck. Head and neck white, with a black eye-stripe extending behind as a crest. Dark blue-black flight feathers and golden iris noticeable on a closer look. Sexes alike. Stands motionless at water's edge, exposed or in water, waiting for prey. Sometimes very cautiously stalks prey, jabbing at it when in reach. Found in freshwaters, backwaters, mangroves and tidal creeks.

Purple Heron *Ardea purpurea* 97cm

Joanna Van Gruisen

A large heron, only slightly smaller than the Grey Heron, but more shy and secretive. Slaty-purple above, white below, with blackish crown and crest, wings and tail, and the stripe on head and neck. Sexes alike but female has crest and plumes less developed. Solitary. Keeps to dense reed cover, or floating hyacinth mats, easily overlooked since it tends to freeze, bittern-like, on suspicion, and due to the blending of the colours with the surroundings. Croaks when disturbed and flushed. It is a resident species. Found in open marshes, reed-covered lakes and riversides.

Toby Sinclair

A close relative of the familiar Pond Heron, but smaller in size and overall black, grey and dark green in colour. Crown black. Head, neck and underparts grey; wings darker, with the quills sort of scalloped. White on cheeks, chin and throat. Immatures more brownish with white underparts streaked with dark brown. Both crepuscular and diurnal; but solitary and shy. Rather silent, keeps to thickets and shrubbery, besides streams and flowing water, jabbing at anything which comes within reach. Tends to flush when almost come upon. Also found in saltwaters.

Indian Pond Heron *Ardeola grayii* 46cm   42

Joanna Van Gruisen

The most ubiquitous of the herons and egrets, the Pond Heron or Paddybird as it is also called, has been quick in colonizing all man-made wetlands, from inundated paddy fields and small ponds to the margins of large reservoirs. Earthy-brown above (more maroonish when breeding), white below, heavily streaked on the breast, with white wings and tail visible in flight. This small, resident heron is inconspicuous when settled but becomes immediately noticeable in a flash of white when it takes wing. Adopts the characteristic wait-and-strike method of the herons and egrets to catch its prey.

S Nagaraj

Frequently come across with grazing cattle, picking up insects disturbed by them and on them. All-white in the non-breeding season; a relatively short yellow beak and yellowish legs. Buffy-orange on head, neck and back when breeding. Sexes alike. A common and widely distributed egret, found in a variety of habitats from wetlands like shorelines, inundated cultivation and floating hyacinth platforms to freshly ploughed land and grasslands. Roosts communally on trees with other similar species. Mostly silent except for some croaking sounds made during breeding times.

Great Egret *Ardea alba* 91cm   46

Joanna Van Gruisen

The biggest amongst the region's white egrets, the Large Egret is less sociable than the others, being usually found as scattered individuals even when in small numbers. The whole bird is lanky, pure white, with the gape extending well behind the eye, and a blackish streak along the gape. During the breeding season, develops diaphanous plumes on the lower back only, and the usually yellow beak turns black. Found on the margins of rivers and lakes, and on mudflats and inundated cultivation like paddy fields. A resident species but subject to local movements.

Little Egret *Egretta garzetta* 63cm 49

T Dalip Singh

One of the smaller, all-white egrets, with black beak and yellow soles for the black legs. In the breeding season develops a thin crest and plumes on the breast and back. Found in a variety of wetland habitats from irrigated fields to shorelines. Found individually or in spread-out groups. Takes a variety of animals for food, from worms and crustaceans, to fish and tadpoles. This species feeds more actively than, for example, the Grey Heron or Large Egret. Flies with steady and slow wingbeats, neck drawn in and legs stretched out.

Pacific Reef Egret *Egretta gularis schistacea* 63cm 50

E Hanumantha Rao

Primarily a bird of saline waters and also found on rocky sea-shores, mangrove swamps, tidal lagoons, and mudflats, the Pacific Reef Egret is dimorphic. There is a white and a dark morph: the general appearance being that of a Little Egret, especially so of the white morph. In the white morph, the bill colour varies from the black of the little egret to being yellowish to horny-brown. The dark morph is bluish-grey all over with white on throat, occasionally a white patch on wings, greenish-yellow bill, olive-green legs and yellow feet. Some authorities treat it as just a race of the Little Egret.

S Nagaraj

A small, relatively short-necked heron with grey, black and white in plumage. Adult has crown to back black tinged with green, wings and sides of body grey, underparts and area around eyes white. A few long, white plumes on head. Coral-red eyes. Young are brown speckled with white. A quack-like '*cwo*' uttered in flight. Roosts and nests quite away from water, even in residential suburbs, in colonies on dense-canopied trees. Commutes to and fro from roosting to feeding grounds at dusk and dawn, becoming also diurnal when breeding, when adults can be seen flying at all times of the day.

Chestnut Bittern *Ixobrychus cinnamomeus* 38cm 56

Kamal Sahai

A nocturnal bird of reed-beds and well-grown, inundated paddy cultivation, the Chestnut Bittern is reddish-brown above, much paler below. Female differs from the male in having the upperparts mottled with dark and light spots, and the underparts streaked darker. Spends the day quietly hidden in some reed-bed, flying out at dusk to feed. It is not at all gregarious, and is usually seen during day when flushed from the roosting sites. General behaviour very much like the common Pond Heron. Found all over India, especially in the south of the Himalayan terai.

Painted Stork *Mycteria leucocephala* 93cm tall
60

An overall white stork, with black and pink in the plumage. Bill yellow and slightly decurved. Breast and wing coverts finely barred black. Pink near tail (which are the closed inner secondaries). Face orange-yellow, main tail and flight features black. Sexes alike. Young pale dirty brown, the neck feathers edged brown and lacks breast band. Usually hunts individually, with partly openbeak immersed in water and probing the bottom sediments. Spends time standing motionless near water or soaring on thermals when fed. Flight direct, with the flight silhouette somewhat hunchbacked.

Asian Openbill *Anastomus oscitans* 81cm   61

The region's smallest stork, this species is overall dirty-white with black flight feathers and a characteristic, long, thick beak, which shows a gap in-between the closed mandibles. The exact function of this gap not known. Sexes alike. Young smoky-brown; darker brown mantle. Essentially a bird of inland waters, found in small flocks. Feeds on molluscs, but also takes other animals like frogs and crabs. Only mandible-clattering and some moaning sounds at nest are heard. A resident species, subject to movements and suspected to have a large post-breeding dispersal.

Woolly-necked Stork *Ciconia episcopus* 106cm tall

Toby Sinclair

A large stork, the size of a White Stork, with a glossy black crown, back, breast and huge wings. Has a white neck, lower abdomen and red legs. The long, stout bill is black, occasionally tinged crimson. Sexes alike. Found in drier areas than most other storks, from flooded grasslands to deep inside forests where marshes occur. Usually not in saline areas. Not gregarious, usually less than about a dozen birds together. Silent, except for the clattering of mandibles with the neck bent over backwards. Like other storks, soars on thermals. Widespread all over the Indian region, up to about 1400m in the Himalayas.

White Stork *Ciconia ciconia* 106cm tall

E Hanumantha Rao

A long-legged, long-necked, egret-like, pure white bird with black flight feathers. Red bill and legs. Sexes alike. Young birds have black parts replaced by brown. One of the two migrant winter visitors amongst the storks in the region. It arrives by mid-September and leaves around end-March. A shy and wary bird, it shares general habits with other storks; feeding on frogs, reptiles, crustaceans, and insects like locusts. Given to soaring on thermals. Silent, except for the clattering of mandibles. Roosts at night on trees. Seen commonly in north-western and central India, and in the Indo-Gangetic plains.

Black-necked Stork *Ephippiorhynchus asiaticus* 135cm tall 66

One of the tallest of the region's storks. Black head, neck and tail, with closed wing also appearing black, but shows off as a black band running diagonally forwards along the wing in flight. Underparts, rest of wing and back white. Coral-red legs. Sexes alike. Solitary or in pairs, feeding in a marsh or perched atop a tree, but shy and wary. Feeds on fish, frogs, lizards, small turtles and insects. Territorial. Given to soaring on thermals as other species. Silent, except for the clattering of mandibles. Though wide-spread in the Indian region, this species is becoming uncommon.

Joanna Van Gruisen

Lesser Adjutant *Leptoptilos javanicus* 130cm tall   67

A large stork with naked dirty-yellowish or reddish head and neck. Upperparts black. Underparts white. A stork of the well-watered tracts, and nowhere common. A resident species subject to seasonal movements. Essentially solitary, but many gather at garbage dumps Takes a variety of animals for food, from crustaceans to snakes, lizards, frogs, fish and small birds, but less of a scavenger than its larger relative, the Greater Adjutant Stork. Silent, except for an occasional loud croak or clattering of bill. Found in marshlands, cultivations, mangroves and in the vicinity of human habitation.

S Nagaraj

Black-headed Ibis *Threskiornis aethiopica* 75cm

S Nagaraj

A gregarious species, the Black-headed Ibis has a naked black head with a white body, black legs and feet. A red or pinkish patch of naked skin along the inner leading edge of underwing, visible in close flight. Sexes alike. Feeds with other birds in the shallows, using its long, decurved beak to probe bottom sediments and ooze for both animal and plant matter. Breeds colonially with other large wading birds like storks, ibises, egrets and herons. Has a loud, booming call but during breeding season, nasal grunts are heard. Though a resident species, it is subject to local movements.

Black Ibis *Pseudibis papillosa* 68cm

T Dalip Singh

A small, dark ibis, rather individualistic. Feeds on drier ground than other ibises. Overall black, with red on the crown of a naked black head and dull red legs. A small white patch on the wing. Sexes alike. Less dependent on water than the Black-headed Ibis. Less gregarious, does not breed in colonies, but as individual pairs well separated from others. Keeps to favoured localities, and roosts in accustomed trees. A loud, nasal screaming cry of two or three notes. General habits and food like other ibises. A resident species, it is commonly seen in north-western India, east through Gangetic plains; south to Mysore.

Joanna Van Gruisen

A small, dark migratory ibis with a feathered head. Head, neck, chin, throat, lower back and rump dark chestnut glossed with green and purple; the head, neck and throat having some white streaks when not breeding. Rest of the plumage glossed with bronze-green and purple. Legs and beak dark greenish. A gregarious species, roosting on trees and tending to fly in a 'V' or a ribbon-like formation. Found in cultivated areas and edges of marshes. When feeding in shallow water, often feeds along with other ibises, storks and spoonbills. Feeds on small fish, frogs, earthworms, insects and crustaceans.

Eurasian Spoonbill *Platalea leucorodia* 83cm   72

E Hanumantha Rao

Hardly confusable with any other species, the Spoonbill has a spatula-shaped, yellow-tipped black bill. The bird is pure white all over, with black legs and a thin black line from base of upper mandible to eyes. In the breeding season develops a long orange-yellow crest and band encircling lower neck and breast; also an orange-red patch on throat. Found in shallow waters of lakes, rivers and marshes, immersing beak in water and moving it from side to side while opening and closing it. Feeds on both animal and vegetable matter. Breeds colonially in mixed heronries. A migrant in the northern part of its range.

Otto Pfister

A distinctive-looking, tall bird of large bodies of water, fresh, brackish estuaries and the sea coast. Long-necked, with long, stilt-like legs, and a characteristic downward-bent beak. Overall rosy white, with scarlet and black wings. Pink beak with black tip. Legs pink. Feeds and breeds gregariously. Feeds in shallow water, beak and head immersed in water upside down with the upper mandible working like a scoop to lift invertebrates from the sediments. Often roosts standing on one leg. A resident species, subject to local movements.

Otto Pfister

Smaller than the Greater Flamingo, this species has a dark beak with crimson feathers around its base. The plumage is also much darker, being rose-pink in colour. The male has crimson on its back and breast which the female lacks. Gregarious, with general habits being similar to the other flamingos. Feeds on algae, including diatoms, by filtration, for which the bill is specially adapted. While immersed in water, it is swung from side to side almost like a hockey stick. In general with flamingos, flocks tend to fly in formation with rapid wing-beats, legs and neck extended out.

Greylag Goose *Anser anser* 81cm

Joanna Van Gruisen

One of the two most common species of geese seen in the region. Visits from end of October, staying on till the middle of March. Gregarious and extremely wary. Its grey-brown plumage, pink bill and feet aid in identification. Sexes alike. Young greyish-brown with brown bill. It normally rests during the day and feeds at night, causing some damage to winter crops. Feeds on minute organisms, molluscs, crustaceans, possibly small fish. Its single-note honk, often repeated, is unmistakable as is its gaggle when feeding. Common in the north, but rarely seen south of Madhya Pradesh.

Bar-headed Goose *Anser indicus* 75cm

S Nagaraj

A fairly common winter visitor and easy to recognize, both because of its size as well as the two prominent black stripes on its white head. Sexes alike. The pale body and yellow bill are further distinguishing marks. Usually found in large groups in the north. Its nasal but musical honking can be heard from afar. The flocks fly in a long, strung-out 'V' formation, and their wild honking is best heard when the birds are flying to or from their feeding grounds. Within India, it breeds in Ladakh, and spreads throughout the region in winter. It is less common in the south of Deccan.

Lesser Whistling-duck *Dendrocygna javanica* 42cm   88

A shallow-water feeder which prefers an abundant growth of weeds and vegetation, it is a small chestnut-brown and maroon-coloured duck with a buff anterior. Chestnut uppertail coverts diagnostic. Has a feeble, flapping, rail-like flight, and broad, rounded wings which, being blackish, appear darker than the rest of the body in flight. A nocturnal feeder avoiding open water, it uses the safety of distance from disturbance, roosting during day and flying out to paddy fields and reed-covered areas to feed during night. Breeds on trees in hollows, forks, and deserted nests of other birds like crows and kites. Has a shrill, whistling, wheezy call in flight.

Ruddy Shelduck *Tadorna ferruginea* 66cm   90

A large, migratory, rusty orange-brown duck with a paler head and neck. Black tail, uppertail coverts and lower half of rump, primaries, bill and legs. Wing with green secondaries and white secondary coverts. Female has a whitish face. Male has a black collar when breeding. Young birds look like female and have some grey in wings. Wary in its winter quarters, and less gregarious than most ducks, found in small numbers roosting on the water's edge, flying out to feed at night. Has a goose-like honk. Breeds in Ladakh and spreads out through the region in winter. Less common in the South.

Pintail *Anas acuta* 56-74cm

S. Nagaraj

Along with the Garganey, one of the most numerous migrant ducks wintering in the Indian region. Underwing grey, with the tail also being longer than in most other ducks.Wintering male andf emale differ in beak colour: the female's being black with grey sides. Overall brown with dark brown markings. In flight, brown speculum with white bar behind it seen on the upperwing. Breeding male handsome with the head and hind-neck chocolate-brown and a partial, white separating line. Back and flanks grey; fore-neck, breast and underparts white. Tail and the associated coverts, black. In flight, green speculum with buff bar distinctive. Found day-roosting on large bodies of water.

Common Teal *Anas crecca* 38cm

Sanctuary / Ranjit Lal

A migrant duck, small in size, with a characteristic emerald-green and black speculum, and a pale wing-bar contributed by the coverts. Upperpart dark brown, feathers paler at the edges; underparts white, with some brown. Lacks the distinctive speculum of the Garganey. Male's breeding plumage distinctive, with head and upper-neck chestnut, and a broad, metallic green band edged with buff lines. Lower neck finely barred with black and white. Underparts white, tail brown; brown, buff and black posteriorly. Gregarious, often found in large aggregations consisting of various other duck species.

S Nagaraj

One of the larger residential ducks, usually found only in small numbers. Overall brown with pale edges to the feathers. Bill black with yellow tip, legs orange-red. A green speculum bordered with black and white; a black and white underwing. Male has a red patch near base of bill. A surface feeder, obtaining its food by up-ending in water or by feeding in marshlands and paddy fields, feeding on seeds, grain and other vegetable matter. Some animal matter also taken. When injured, dives and remains underwater with only bill exposed. Generally silent. A resident species, subject to local movements.

Mallard *Anas platyrhynchos* 61cm 100

E Hanumantha Rao

A surface-feeding large migrant duck with dimorphic sexes. Female and non-breeding male brown with the feathers edged with buff, the buff more prominent below. A purplish-blue speculum bordered anteriorly and posteriorly with white. Orange-red legs. The non-breeding male has a yellowish beak. Male in breeding plumage has a green head, brown breast, a black posterior, and a greyish-white body. A gregarious dabbling species, keeping usually in small parties. Wary; day-roosts on the water, flying out to feed in marshes and paddy fields at night. Flies well, taking off easily from the water.

Gadwall *Anas strepera* 51cm

Joanna Van Gruisen

A dull-plumaged, plain-looking migrant duck, brown in colour with dark brown markings; black bill with well-defined orange-yellow sides. White secondaries and black greater wing coverts form the speculum; and in the breeding male, additional contrasting chestnut median wing coverts. The breeding male is a grey-brown bird with black bill, paler face, white belly and a dark posterior, the breast also being darker with black, crescent-shaped markings. General habits and behaviour like the Mallard, this species also being a surface feeder or a dabbling duck.

Garganey *Anas querquedula* 38cm

104

R K Gaur

One of the most abundant and widespread of our ducks, this migrant has a rather prominent dark eye-band and a pale oval patch at base of bill during winters. In the non-breeding season, both sexes overall dullish brown, scalloped paler. Speculum dull green (brighter in male) enclosed between two white bands. Whitish eyebrow and stripe below eye-band. Throat white. Breeding male has upperparts brown with prominent, broad, white supercilium, brown breast and white belly. Found in almost any still body of water, sleeping over the surface, head tucked into the feathers of the back, or sometimes feeding, up-ending in water. Flies out at dusk to feed elsewhere.

Northern Shoveler *Anas clypeata* 51cm

Joanna Van Gruisen

A common winter visitor. Has a characteristically broadened and lengthened beak and orange-red legs. Overall mottled dark brown and buff with greyish-blue shoulder patch and white-bordered, green speculum. The non-breeding male has a blackish head, while the breeding male has the head and neck black, the latter tinged with green; flanks and belly chestnut; undertail coverts black and a lot of white in the plumage. A filter feeder, sieving the watery ooze for all forms of animal and vegetable matter, swimming with the lower mandible immersed in water, occasionally up-ending in water, but never diving.

Cotton Pygmy-goose *Nettapus coromandelianus* 33cm 114

G & H Denzau

The smallest of the region's ducks, with white predominating in the plumage. A mainly vegetarian duck with a goose-like bill, keeping to the weedy portions of the water. Male has a glossy greenish-black back, a low greenish-black collar and a blackish-brown crown; rest white. The female has a brown crown and eye-stripe; face and neck finely speckled and barred with brown; upperparts, wings and tail brown; rest white. A fast flier, uttering a crackling note on the wing. Clumsy on land and trusts man where not molested.

Comb Duck *Sarkidiornis melanotos* 76cm

S Nagaraj

A resident duck, goose-like and large, glossy black dorsally and white ventrally. Head and neck white speckled with black. A black half-collar down side of white breast. Flanks greenish. Male in the breeding season has a greatly swollen fleshy knob at the base of the bill. Female is duller, smaller and lacks the knob. Found in bodies of water with surrounding tree cover. Has a goose-like honk in the breeding season. Also perches on trees, building a nest in tree hollows. Mostly resident but moves considerably with onset of monsoons. Feeds on shoots and seeds of water plants, grain, aquatic insects, worms and frogs.

Common Merganser *Mergus merganser* 66cm

Otto Pfister

A fish-eating, diving duck with a beak having a hooked tip and serrated edges, this is a bird of large bodies of water, both still and flowing. Locally fairly common, occurring mainly in winter. Greyish-brown above, white below, with the head and neck rufous, sharply demarcated from the body. Female has a short crest, and the non-breeding male (described above) has a white line from lores to beak. A prominent white speculum. Tends to fly low over water. Often hunts fish co-operatively as in cormorants. Ungainly on land, but an expert swimmer and diver.

Black-shouldered Kite *Elanus caeruleus* 33cm   124

T Dalip Singh

An elegant, pigeon-sized, long-winged hawk of a savanna-type habitat: grasslands and cultivation interspersed with trees. Head, neck and underparts white. Upperparts pale ashy-grey. A black eye-patch, crimson eyes, and black shoulder patches. Wings long, extending beyond tail when closed. Tail square. Immatures have upper-body brown, with pale edges to feathers. Pounces on prey spotted from a lookout perch, or when flying. Hovers frequently, being quite steady when doing so. Roosts communally, in well-foliaged trees. Feeds on locusts, other insects and small animals of its habitat.

Oriental Honey-Buzzard *Pernis ptilorhyncus* 68cm   130

T Dalip Singh

One of the few birds specialized in preying on bee colonies, especially on the large rock bee, the Oriental Honey-Buzzard has the head completely feathered, including the lores. This species is about the size of the common Pariah Kite, with a short, nuchal crest when seen in profile and a smallish, pigeon-like head. Plumage colour variable: upperparts from buffish to almost black; underparts pale brown barred with white. Tail usually banded. Usually seen gliding in pairs or individually, or perched on a treetop. Found in areas with trees, from forest to cultivated land: usually where rock bees could occur.

Krupakar Senani

A common commensal of man, overall brown, the head paler and the wings darker. A black eye-patch. A diagnostic forked tail with numerous dark crossbars on close look. Body feathers edged paler. Gregarious, roosting communally. Seen in most Indian towns and cities, scavenging and occasionally snatching food, including eatables like sandwiches. A bird of easy flight, manoeuvring adroitly even in the most congested of thoroughfares, swooping down to pick up a dead rat or the like, without even a slightest hint of a collision. Call a shrill musical '*wheehehehehehe*' squeal.

Brahminy Kite *Haliastur indus* 48cm   135

Vivek Sinha

A handsome-looking and common bird which is frequently seen around water and is only slightly smaller than the familiar Pariah Kite. Its white head, neck, upper back and breast contrast well with the rich, rusty chestnut of rest of the plumage. The abdomen is more brownish. Feeds on crabs, fish, frogs and such-like animals found in and around water, sick birds, as big as ducks, often scooped up in a graceful sweeping dive. Usually silent, but has a call similar to, but distinct from, that of the Pariah Kite. Found on margins of lakes, marshes, rivers and sea coast.

Shikra *Accipiter badius* 31-36cm   139

E Hanumantha Rao

A daring, pigeon-sized small hawk of well-wooded country. One of the most common hawks to be found in the region, it is pale ashy-grey above, white below, finely barred with rusty-brown, especially on the breast. A median grey stripe on the throat. Female larger; immatures brown above and boldly streaked with brown below. Wings short and rounded; tail is long and barred. A cat of the bird world, the Shikra hunts by almost ambushing its prey. The flight is swift: a few rapid wing-strokes followed by a glide; the bird invariably flies up into a tree to alight on a branch. Captures any animal of manageable size, but no carrion. Given to soaring on thermals. Has a challenging call.

White-eyed Buzzard *Butastur teesa* 43cm   157

E Hanumantha Rao

A Jungle-Crow-sized, greyish-brown hawk of open forest, scrub and cultivation in the dry zones of the Indian region. A white throat and nape patch; pale eyes. Orangish-yellow cere and legs. Dark chin and cheek stripes. Wings are long, broad and rounded, typically buzzard like. In overhead flight, underwing looks paler than body. Sedentary in habits, looking out for prey from a vantage point day in and day out. The lookout perch could be anything: tree stumps, treetops, telegraph poles, even earthen mounds. Becomes very active during the breeding season, especially during courtship.

Changeable Hawk Eagle *Spizaetus cirrhatus* 72cm 161

Krupakar Senani

A slim and powerful kite-sized raptor of forested habitats. Brown above, brown streaked white below, the streaks starting as fine markings on the throat and becoming thicker and bolder on breast. A black sagittal crest and long, feathered legs distinctive. More of a large hawk than an eagle, even in looks, sweeping down and ambushing prey. Sits on a high perch on the top of some well-foliaged tree and keeps a keen lookout for animals moving down below. Preys on hares, large birds like junglefowl, partridges, quails; squirrels, lizards and the like. Has a loud, high-pitched call, starting short and ending in a scream: more often heard in the breeding season.

Steppe Eagle *Aquila rapax nipalensis* 76-80cm 169

E Hanumantha Rao

A large variable coloured brown migratory eagle. Plumage colour ranges from blackish to a pale buffish-brown. Whitish tips to secondaries and its coverts contribute the two wingbars, visible both on the upper and underwings. Has a patch of rufous on nape sometimes. Sexes alike, female slightly larger. Solitary or several scattered, it obtains its food by piracy, by eating carrion, and also by pouncing on small animals that come by. Utters loud crackling notes; high-pitched call. Has a lazy, low flight. A winter visitor, it is found in open country, vicinities of villages, towns and areas of cultivation.

Joanna Van Gruisen

A distinctive-looking large bird of prey of the peninsular seaboard, ashy-brown above and pure white on the head, neck, underparts and terminal third of tail. Sexes alike; female larger. When gliding, long wings held above line of body. Wedge-shaped tail distinctive. Invariably in pairs, gliding regally along the shoreline beyond the surf zone; or perched on some vantage point. Feeds on sea snakes, fish and other animals picked up in a neat sweep and devoured at some favourite perch. Noisy in the breeding season: often duetting. Found on sea coasts and inland water especially the coast south of Bombay and all along the east coast.

Pallas's Fish Eagle *Haliaeetus leucoryphus* 76-84cm   174

Joanna Van Gruisen

A huge eagle of the larger north Indian rivers and reservoirs. Dark brown above and below, golden-brown to fulvous head and neck. Tail with broad dark terminal and a broad, white subterminal band; rounded and not usually spread. Female larger. A typical eagle, adapted to feeding on fish in wetland habitats. Uses a mound, fishing stake or a waterside tree to keep a lookout for fish; also feeds on large birds, snakes, frogs and carrion (including corpses), or flies about for the same. Obtains its food frequently by robbing other birds of prey of their booty.

A plains vulture of medium size, the Red-headed Vulture has the head and neck bare, thighs and legs pinkish-red; with a flat, pendant wattle behind each ear. White patches on upper thighs and at base of neck; white band along underwing visible in flight. Wings held above line of body. Young are darkish brown with white abdomen and undertail. Rather timid and unsocial, found in ones and twos at carcasses waiting for the jostling to reduce to have a tug at the flesh, withdrawing when the competition increases. Builds a large, platform-nest of sticks and twigs on some large tree, and if unavailable as in a semi-desert, even on bushes.

Long-billed Vulture *Gyps indicus* 92cm 182

A large, resident vulture, light to dark brown above, with paler edges to feathers, and very pale brown below. A ruff of white feathers at the base of the neck; head and neck patchily covered with whitish down. Sexes alike. Distinguished from the White-rumped Vulture by the back being brown and, when flying overhead, by the different underwing pattern: wing quills black and rest of underwing pale brown merging with the colour of ventral body. Sociable and silent. General habits same as other vultures. Commonly seen in the drier parts of India like Rajasthan, Gujarat and most of Central India.

White-rumped Vulture *Gyps bengalensis* 90cm 185

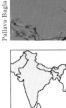

A widespread vulture and perhaps the most common of the large vultures. Overall brownish-black with the lower back white. A whitish ruff of feathers at base of neck, broken in the front. Gives a hunchbacked impression when perched, a graceful steadiness when sailing. Distinguished from the Long-billed in overhead flight by the pale leading edge of underwing contrasting with the dark wing quills and dark ventral side of the body. Upper flanks and thigh coverts white. Gregarious; roosting and nesting in groups. A carrion feeder, hardly ever takes any live prey. Produces a few rough screeches.

Egyptian Vulture *Neophron percnopterus* 66cm 186

The smallest vulture in the region, being about the size of the common Pariah Kite. Overall white, with a relatively short, naked neck, head and bill yellow. Legs pale flesh. Main flight feathers black; tail wedge-shaped. Sexes alike. A bird of open country, and not usually gregarious. Apart from carrion, scavenges around village outskirts and garbage dumps; also takes small animals and large insects. Builds a platform-nest on edges of cliffs and buildings. Found in open country and in the vicinity of human habitation. Widespread and locally common.

Photo credits: Pallava Bagla (top), Joanna Van Gruisen (bottom)

Eurasian Marsh Harrier *Circus aeruginosas* 54-59cm 193

Kamal Sahai

The largest of the region's harriers, and one of the early winter migrants to arrive, the Eurasian Marsh Harrier can be seen frequenting wet ground and wetland areas. The pale rufous head, neck and breast look distinct from the dark brown of the rest of the body. Female is dark chocolate-brown, with a buff head cap and buff leading edge to proximal end of wing. Easily distinguished from the slightly larger Pariah Kite by the rounded, not forked, tail. More common in the North, though seen throughout the Indian region. Found on marshes and wet cultivation. Feeds on fish, rodents and frogs.

Crested Serpent Eagle *Spilornis cheela* 74cm 196

Joanna Van Gruisen

A large, forest raptor, having white-spotted brown underparts, the brown being the same shade dorsally. Cere, legs, feet and irises yellow. A prominent, pied, transversely oriented, fan-like, nuchal crest. Underwing pattern distinctive: a broad white band in-between a pair of broad black bands on the main flight feathers, preceded with a few more black and white bands anteriorly. Tail has two broad black bands with an intervening white band. Often seen soaring over the forest canopy, the bird itself a minute speck in the heavens. The shrill, piercing cry draws attention well before bird is visible.

G & H Denzau

A migratory, kite-sized raptor found near large bodies of water. Contrasting dark brown upperparts and pure white underparts and head. A dark brown breast band and a dark stripe running along the eye. Sexes alike. In overhead flight, wing tips and carpal patches darker; white underparts and breast band clearly visible; also the squarish tail. Catches fish by plunging into water, the fish being taken later to a perch to be devoured. Seen perched on a stake or a tree, or flying about, sometimes hovering to take a better look. Usually silent in its winter quarters.

Peregrine Falcon *Falco peregrinus* 40-48cm   209

Asad Rahmani

A typical streamlined falcon, dark ashy-grey above and fulvous-white below. Conspicuous black cheek stripe and finely dark-barred underparts. Jungle-Crow-sized and usually found individually. Captures prey, usually waterfowl, in a fast dive, raking the prey with its hind-claw. Flight direct and powerful, a few fast wing-deep beats followed by a glide. Like other falcons, spends a lot of time waiting for prey from a vantage perch. Found near wetlands. Eats a wide variety of bird species. Has a fairly loud, ringing scream.

Sanctuary / G & H Denzau

A dove-sized falcon of open, wooded country and a savanna-type habitat. Sexes alike with the female being larger. Slaty-grey above with darker head and cheek-stripe. Underparts reddish-white, streaked with black and with the thighs and undertail coverts more rufous. Diurnal and crepuscular, feeding on small birds and small bats, as well as large flying insects, which are devoured on the wing. Flies about in wide arcs, raising and falling in height, attacking flying prey in a swift, downward swoop. Calls and general habits similar to those of other falcons.

Common Kestrel *Falco tinnunculus* 36cm   222

Amarjeet Singh

A dove-sized falcon of open country, well-known for its habit of hovering. Head grey streaked darker, with a characteristic dark cheek-stripe. Grey rump, uppertail coverts and tail. Lower plumage rufous-buff with breast and flanks streaked and spotted with brown. Tail white-tipped, with a black subterminal band. Female larger and brownish-rufous above. Underparts with bolder markings than the male. Tail barred; with white tip and dark subterminal band. Both sexes have wing-tips darker. A bird of open country, feeds on insects, lizards and small rodents which it captures by plummetting down.

Joanna Van Gruisen

A red-legged, medium-sized partridge with uniform upperparts, found in barren or open mountainsides, could very well be this species. Prominent rib-like bands on flanks. Upperparts pinkish-olive. A black band which runs across forehead and eyes meets on breast, enclosing bright white cheeks and throat. Female slightly smaller; lacks spur on tarsus. Keeps together in family groups and occasionally in larger numbers. The group scatters when flushed, the birds being fast on the wing, but tending to run before they take flight. The name is from the call of the bird, being onomatopoeic.

Black Francolin *Francolinus francolinus* 34cm   238

R K Gaur

A partridge of tall grass and cultivation in well-watered tracts, as well as tea plantations in the Himalayan foothills. Male is jet-black, boldly spotted and marked with white; scalloped with fulvous above; with prominent white cheeks, chestnut neck, belly and undertail coverts. Female browner, and lacks the chestnut on neck and white cheek patches. Has off-white chin and throat. Like other partridges, is more active in the mornings and evenings and less so at midday. Has a habit of carrying its tail up like the moorhen, when sauntering out of cover while feeding.

Painted Francolin *Francolinus pictus* 31cm

A black-coloured partridge, heavily patterned with white, found in grassland and cultivation interspersed with bush and scrub. Brownish-black above, black below; spotted, barred and scalloped with white above, very boldly spotted with white below. Rufous on abdomen and vent; chestnut on supercilium, face and throat. In flight, heavily spotted plumage and rich rufous in wing distinctive. A shy bird being more active during mornings and evenings, and less so during the midday. Prefers wetter areas than the Grey, but drier areas than the Black Francolin.

Grey Francolin *Francolinus pondicerianus* 33cm

An overall light greyish-brown ground bird of thorny scrub and scattered cultivation – drier than that preferred by other partridges. Upperparts heavily patterned with buff and black mottling, bars and vermiculations. Underparts buff with dark vermiculations and bars. Sexes alike. Chin and throat rufous-buff enclosed within a blackish gorget. In the non-breeding season, found in small family flocks that scatter when disturbed, some running and some flying. Chestnut tail noticeable in flight. Noisy; utters a loud, high-pitched two- to three-note '*pat-ee-la*'.

Swamp Francolin *Francolinus gularis* 37cm

Vivek Menon

Larger than the other partridges, this species prefers swampy grasslands subject to seasonal flooding. Brown and rufous-brown above, barred with buff; supercilium and a broad band below eye buff. Underparts brown, with black-bordered, bold white streaks. Chin, throat and fore-neck rusty red. Wades across in swampy water, clambering up stems to cross if water too deep. Very reluctant to fly, preferring to run instead. Violent fights between males often leave scars on neck and breast.

Jungle Bush Quail *Perdicula asiatica* 17cm

E Hanumantha Rao

One of the more common species of an endemic genus, and found in grass and scrub of deciduous and secondary forests. Upperparts buffish-brown streaked and mottled darker. A buff and chestnut supercilium extending as a stripe down sides of neck. Underparts white barred black in male, pinkish-rufous with bright chestnut throat patch in female. Found in small flocks or coveys, which rest bunched together with all individuals facing outward, and move about trooping one behind another. The covey tends to 'explode' from almost under one's foot, the individuals scattering in all directions and regrouping later through soft calls.

Himalayan Monal *Lophophorus impejanus* 72cm

Joanna Van Gruisen

A species of Himalayan pheasant, found in high-altitude forest edge and open forest, between 2600m and 5000m, moving up and down within this range depending on season. Female overall brown, shaped like the male but with a shorter crest, motted and patterned all over. Has a white throat. White in tail prominent in flight. Male black below with metallic green head and crest turning metallic purple on sides of neck and wing coverts. Wing quills black, rump white, uppertail coverts metallic green, tail rufous-chestnut. A whistling call in flight; flies into trees when flushed and freezes.

Kalij Pheasant *Lophura leucomelana* 60-68cm

Sumit Sen

A member of the Silver Pheasant group, this species is found in thick undergrowth of steep mountainside forests, usually near water. Male glossy black above, brownish-grey below. Rump feathers edged with white; also some white below. Tail long and drooping at tip. Crest long and black in the nominate race. A bare red patch around eye. Female like male but reddish-brown with paler scalloping and stiff tail. A typical pheasant and close relative of the junglefowls. Wanders about on to open ground to feed on seed and grain, but never too far from cover. Has various chuckles and clucks, uttered by both male and female.

Joanna Van Gruisen

This species is the ancestor of all domestic poultry and is found in forests, and cultivation bordering forests, in north and eastern India, roughly coinciding with the distribution of the Sal Tree, *Shorea robusta*. Male glossy deep orange-red and yellow above; blackish-brown below. Laterally flattened black tail with lengthened and arched central tail feathers. Female overall reddish-brown, the redness varying on different parts, with the feathers of the neck tipped yellow, and uniform underparts. Found in small groups; very shy and wild: the consequence of much persecution by man.

E Hanumantha Rao

Ashy and timid endemic junglefowl of peninsular India, found in bamboo jungles, abandoned plantations with thickets, and secondary forests. Male overall dark grey, with darker main tail and flight feathers. Feathers of neck and mantle spotted with orange-yellow; those of breast white-streaked. Tail distinctly longer than Red's. Neck feathers duller, tail shorter and comb reduced when not breeding. Female smaller, without comb, brown above and streaked paler; white below. Feathers scalloped paler dorsally and darker ventrally. Much persecuted and hence very shy, but bolder where unmolested by man. Male has a characteristic '*kuk-ka-kurra-kuk*' call.

Indian Peafowl *Pavo cristatus* F86cm; Ml10cm
including train 2.25m.

E Hanumantha Rao

A huge, crested ground bird of deciduous forests; introduced and in a semi-feral state in many other habitats. A distinctive crest having the feathers broadened terminally, and enormously lengthened uppertail coverts. Male has neck and breast pale blue-green and a bronze-green ocellated train. Primaries and wing coverts pale chestnut, secondaries black. Female smaller, overall brown, more rufous on head, and metallic green on neck. Keeps together in small flocks, trusting their legs rather than their wings for escape. Roosts at night in trees. Call distinctive and far-carrying: a loud '*may-aw*'.

Common Crane *Grus grus* 140cm tall   320

E Hanumantha Rao

A pale greyish-brown, large crane of open country and cultivation. A dull red patch on nape. Black of head and neck divided by a broad white stripe which runs behind and down from the eye all along the neck. Tail concealed by a mass of drooping curly plumes. Bill greenish-yellow and legs black. In flight there is a sharp contrast between the black flight feathers and grey wing coverts. Found in grasslands, farmlands, lakes and rivers. Gregarious and migratory. Roosts standing massed beside water, flying out in the mornings and evenings to feed in the fields.

Black-necked Crane *Grus nigricollis* 156cm tall   321

Ashok Dilwali

A rare crane of swampy land having a very restricted distribution within the area. Tall and overall white, with the head, neck, and all flight feathers black, the last especially noticeable in flight. Lores and crown naked and dull red; a small white patch behind eye. Immatures slightly smaller, overall paler and with the head and neck brownish. A species endemic to the Tibetan Plateau. Found in high-altitude marshes, lakesides, open cultivation. Feeds on fallen grain, shoots, tubers, insects and possibly molluscs. Can be heard trumpeting before migration in February–March.

Sarus Crane *Grus antigone* 156cm tall   323

E Hanumantha Rao

The largest crane in the region and one of the largest birds in India. The Sarus is overall pale grey with a naked red head and upper neck. Bill pale with dark tip, legs and feet red. Young birds are brownish-grey, with the whole head and neck covered with rusty buff feathers. The only resident crane in the region, the Sarus haunts open country, marshland and water. Normally found in pairs, the individuals pairing for life. Apart from the vegetarian diet usual to cranes, takes a lot of fish. Loud, far-reaching, trumpeting cry, often a duet between a pair.

Siberian Crane *Grus leucogeranus* 140cm tall

Vivek Sinha

A tall, elegant white crane, migratory and endangered. Bare red skin on forehead, fore-crown and around eye. Primaries and primary coverts black, seen when flying. Long, thick bill and legs pink. In the immatures, upperparts are yellowish-brown. Bharatpur Sanctuary in India has been the main wintering site for the western population. A largely vegetarian crane feeding on various parts of aquatic plants. Consequently found wading into water more than other cranes. A vocal bird; its loud trumpeting calls may be heard in winter too; a musical '*koonk…koonk…*' cry heard while in flight.

Demoiselle Crane *Anthropoides virgo* 76cm tall   326

E Hanumantha Rao

The smallest of the region's cranes, and also perhaps the most widely distributed in India, albeit in winter. An ashy-grey crane with the face and neck black. Black plumes dangling from foreneck and breast. White plumes behind eye and elongated black tertials drooping over tail when wing closed. Primaries, primary coverts and secondaries also black. Bill olive-grey with pink tip. Sexes alike. Shares general habits with the Common Crane with which it co-occurs, even migrating together. Feeds early mornings and early evenings in cultivation; rests during hot hours on marsh-edges and sandbanks.

White-breasted Waterhen *Amaurornisphoenicurus* 32cm 343

E Hanumantha Rao

Often found in parks and neighbourhood of villages in addition to its normal habitat of reedy marshlands and edges of water. Upperparts ashy-grey except for forehead, supercilia, and sides of head which are pale white like most of the underparts. Undertail coverts, vent and flanks rufous. Some grey on breast. Wanders about under shrubbery and hedges, clambering up the bases of thorny bamboo clumps, and shrubs. Any wet place with cover, including grasslands are not out of bounds for this rail. Has a '*kwak*' or '*kwok*' call and a '*krr-kwaak-kwaak*' song repeated rapidly.

Common Moorhen *Gallinula chloropus* 32cm 347

Amarjeet Singh

A slaty-grey bird of well-vegetated, reed-bordered ponds and lakes. Upperparts more brownish, with a white line along flanks. Undertail coverts white. Bill and frontal shield red, with the bill tip yellow. Iris red, legs greenish. Immatures more brownish, with more white in underparts, and brown bill. Scattered individuals or small groups near reed beds. Rides high while swimming, bobbing head. Flicks tail to reveal white undertail typically like a rail, which is especially noticeable when walking on land. Feeds on seeds and tubers of water plants, insects, molluscs, small fish and frogs.

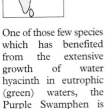

Joanna Van Gruisen

One of those few species which has benefited from the extensive growth of water hyacinth in eutrophic (green) waters, the Purple Swamphen is found in good numbers in such habitats. Overall purplish-blue with long red legs and much lengthened toes. Bill and frontal shield (casque) red. Flight feathers black with the exposed portions blue. White undertail. Separated individuals or groups on floating hyacinth and other aquatic plants, or in reed-beds. Flicks tail typically like a rail, flashing the white underneath. Frequently seen chasing each other in the breeding season. Much persecuted by man in some places.

Common Coot *Fulica atra* 42cm   350

Joanna Van Gruisen

Often seen swimming about on the water like a dark duck, the Coot can very easily be distinguished by its pointed ivory-white beak and white frontal shield. Legs dark greyish-green, with the toes lobed. The Coot is more aquatic than the other members of its rail family, and is usually seen feeding or swimming in the open waters. Gregarious and usually in loosely knit flocks; when disturbed has a habit of half flying, half running, pattering on the surface of the water and moving away and flopping on to the water once again.

Indian Bustard *Choriotis nigriceps* M122cm, F92cm

Joanna Van Gruisen

Found in open country with thin grassland, cultivation and scrub interspersed together. Female similar to male but smaller. Light sandy-brown above with black crown and crest, and white underparts with black gorget across lower breast. Female has the head and neck vermiculated with black and the breast band variable. Occurs in small numbers, rather scattered, and is very shy and wary. Runs fast and carries the body horizontal. Flies with rhythmic flapping of the wings and the legs tucked in. Feeds on grain, seeds, tubers; also insects, rodents, snakes and lizards. Utters a loud '*whonk*' cry, often audible for over a mile. An endangered species.

Bengal Florican *Eupodotis bengalensis* 66cm; 55cm tall 356

Joanna Van Gruisen

Rather individualistic but every bit a bustard, the Bengal Florican is found in tall grassland with scattered bushes and scrub. Sexes dimorphic. Male overall black with brown back heavily patterned with black. Exposed portions of closed wing show up as a white patch. Elongated feathers on head (crest) and breast. Female overall buff, varying in shade on different parts, mottled and patterned with black on back. No white patch on wings. Face paler. Crown darker with a bold buff coronal stripe. A good runner, a good flier, and very wary. Runs on alighting: thus increasing distance from observer.

Pheasant-tailed Jacana *Hydrophasianus chirurgus* 31cm
without tail 358

Found in floating, vegetation-covered bodies of water, walking lightly over the mass of leaves. The male is long-tailed when breeding and short-tailed when not. Chocolate-brown above and below, with a golden-yellow hind-neck, white face, fore-neck, breast and wing (except primaries which are black). Yellow and white separated by a black line. In the non-breeding season, the dark belly turns white, leaving a dark breast band. The enormously lengthened toes distribute its weight and enables 'lily trotting'. Shows the same flash of white when it takes wing like a Pond Heron, becoming inconspicuous on alighting.

Bronze-winged Jacana *Metopidius indicus* 28-31cm 359

One of the two lily-trotters found in this region. Unmistakable because of its long legs and massive toes, the glistening bronze-green back and wings, the latter especially so when they catch the sun. Also has a broad white stripe over the eyes. Seen in small groups in the non-breeding season. Pairs just before the monsoon. Extremely wary and flies low with legs trailing. Lays eggs on large floating leaves in dense vegetation of the ponds it frequents. Utters a harsh note and also a shrill piping call. Found on vegetation-covered ponds, it feeds on tubers, seeds of aquatic plants and also insects, crustaceans, molluscs.

57

White-tailed Lapwing (Plover) *Vanellus leucurus* 28cm362

Joanna Van Gruisen

Looking rather like a Yellow-wattled Lapwing without the black cap on the head, the White-tailed Lapwing is a bird which frequents the marshy grassland margins of large bodies of water. Brown above and grey on chin, throat and breast. Forehead, supercilium and belly whitish. In flight, white rump, uppertail coverts and tail noticeable, as also the bold black primaries and white underwing pattern. Long yellow legs. No wattles. Gregarious: in winter associates with other waders like Redshanks in small groups. Tends to lift up both wings back to back, now and again, as a signal between roosting individuals.

Red-wattled Lapwing *Vanellus indicus* 33cm   366

Joanna Van Gruisen

This handsome plover is one of the more common birds, seen both in the vicinity of cities as well as in the fields. Its jet-black head, neck and breast contrasts with the rest of the plumage. The mantle is bronze-brown, while the belly is white; a white band on either side of the neck continues upwards towards the eyes. It has a crimson wattle which gives it its name. Sexes alike. Its '*did-you-do-it?*' call is one of the most familiar in India. Seen usually in pairs. Is extremely wary of intruders, raising an excited alarm on the slightest threat of danger. Feeds on insects, seeds and tubers during mornings and late into evenings. Widespread.

Yellow-wattled Lapwing *Vanellus malabaricus* 27cm

Vivek Sinha

A plover of dry open country. Light brown above, and on throat and breast. Black crown, chin, and wing quills. A thin black line separates the brown from the white of abdomen. A thin white line demarcates the black crown. Wattle yellow, as are the legs. Sexes alike. Rather quiet, and less noisy than the Red-wattled. Has a '*did-did-did*' call, easily distinguishable from its relatives'. Unlike the Red-wattled, which likes the neighbourhood of water, the Yellow-wattled Lapwing prefers drier open country, keeping together in pairs or small flocks. Moves suspiciously; feeding mostly on insects.

Little Ringed Plover *Charadrius dubius* 17cm   380

E. Hanumantha Rao

Found on the mudbanks of bodies of water, this species is brown above and white below, with a black band which is forked in the front, running across the eye and enclosing a small white patch on the forehead. A black collar on the upper breast runs along a white band on the sides and back of the neck. Throat and chin white. No wing bar visible in flight; yellow legs and yellow ring around eye are additional pointers. In the non-breeding season, black is replaced by brown, and the breast band may be broken. Utters a '*few-few*' whistle, high-pitched but somewhat plaintive. Seemingly scattered individuals take flight together when disturbed.

Eurasian Curlew *Numenius arquata* 58cm   388

Getting its onomatopoeic name from its un-forgettable call, the Eurasian Curlew keeps to large bodies of water, preferring saltwater and the sea such as tidal mudflats, backwaters, estuaries, and the like. Long down-curved beak prominent. Overall sandy-brown, paler below, fading to white posteriorly; scalloped with fulvous above and streaked with black below. Lower back; rump, uppertail coverts, underwing, and posterior abdomen white. No white bar on upperwing. Wing tips darker. Found singly or in small groups running about and probing the ooze and crab holes. Runs before it takes off. Wary and fast on the wing.

Black-tailed Godwit *Limosa limosa* 40cm   389

A migratory wader of marshes and occasionally estuaries and creeks, sandy-brown above, whitish below, and having a straight, uncurved, lengthy beak which is black at the tip and pink towards the base. A prominent white wing bar on upperwing visible in flight; also a black terminal band to white tail and rump. Dark legs project much beyond tail in flight. Found feeding or standing on flooded land; searches for food by probing bill right into the mud and ooze, sometimes even getting its head submerged in water. Generally silent; has a three-syllabled call when flushed.

Joanna Van Gruisen

A large, migratory sandpiper running about and feeding on swampy shorelines. Has orange-red legs and beak, the latter black-tipped. Greyish-brown above, with white lower back, rump, tail and underparts. Breast finely streaked with brown. White of back and trailing edge to wing noticeable in flight, as are the red legs projecting beyond the tail. In summer, browner above, marked black and fulvous and more heavily streaked below. Feeds on aquatic insects, crustaceans, molluscs. A three-noted, Greenshank-like call. When alarmed or suspicious, bobs its head and posterior violently up and down, typical of sandpipers.

Greenshank *Tringa nebularia* 36cm   396

David Cottridge

The largest of the sandpipers, the Greenshank is migratory like others of the group. White predominates in the plumage, with the forehead, lowerback, rump, tail and underparts being of this colour. Rest of the upperparts dark greyish-brown, with the tail having very faint dark barring. Legs are dark and the bill slightly upcurved. There is no wingbar on the upperwing. Underwing is white. Distinguished from the Marsh Sandpiper (Little Greenshank) by the bill shape, and in being closer to the Black-winged Stilt in size. Flushing call is a three-noted *'teu-teu-teu'*. Feeds on crustaceans, molluscs, aquatic insects. Found in marshes, estuaries and creeks.

Wood Sandpiper *Tringa glareola* 21cm

Easily distinguished from the other smaller sandpipers by the larger spots on upperparts. Greyish-brown above with large whitish spots; lower back, rump and tail white; the tail barred with blackish. Less contrasting white rump and brown back compared to the Green. Underparts white, breast darker. A distinct white supercilium extending to behind eye. No wing bar. Legs pale greenish. Gregarious, aggregating to quite decent numbers. A typical sandpiper, wading into water and probing with bill. Call is a quick repeated '*chip-chip-chip*'; and a shrill '*pee-pee-pee*' when flushed. It is a winter visitor to most of India.

Joanna Van Gruisen

Common Sandpiper *Tringa hypoleucos* 21cm

Ashish Chandola

One of the smaller sandpipers preferring stony or rocky margins of irrigation tanks and other bodies of water, including seashores and creeks. Olive-brown above including the rump. White-edged brown tail. White below with a diffuse darker breast band. White supercilium. In flight, the white wing bar and the white edging to tail clearly visible. The white of the lower breast intrudes as a small white edging to the closed wing. Not gregarious, being usually found singly. Because of the firmer ground which it prefers, tends to pick up food rather than probe with its bill. A shrill '*tee-tee-tee*' when flushed.

Common Fantail Snipe *Gallinago gallinago* 27cm   409

The Fantail Snipe is dark brown above, heavily streaked and scalloped with black, rufous and buff, and whitish below. Upperbreast streaked, flanks thereafter barred. In flight distinguished from others by the conspicuous white trailing edge to secondaries and inner primaries; also by largely white underwing coverts. Has a short flushing note when it takes off. Rather short-legged and longer-beaked than sandpipers, snipe in the field are rather inconspicuous, staying under cover in marsh vegetation, or being obliterated against the marshy ground because of the camouflaging colouration.

Black-winged Stilt *Himantopus himantopus* 25cm   430

In this region, very few species can ever be confused with the Black-winged Stilt. A long-legged black and white bird found wading into the shallows till almost belly-deep. Almost never found away from water. The long bill is black in colour and the stilt-like legs crimson. Wings, both above and below, and back are black. Head, neck, rump and tail white, the last suffused with grey. Gregarious, tending to form pure flocks. Has a curious high-stepping gait when wading. Even submerges head in water when feeding. Utters shrill notes in flight, very tern-like; is more noisy when it is breeding.

G & H Denzau

A trim black and white pied plumage, with long thin beak and legs, the former clearly upcurved and the latter quite blue in colour, give the Avocet its distinctiveness. Eyes red. Pairs or small groups wading into the shallows or occasionally even swimming in water. Wields the beak like a hockey stick when wading, disturbing the bottom sediments and picking up small water invertebrates for food. When swimming in water, often up-ends like a dabbling duck in the process of reaching the bottom. A clear, soft '*kluit*' or '*klooit*' call uttered many times in succession when on the wing.

Eurasian Thick-knee *Burhinus oedicnemus* 41cm   436

S Nagaraj

A nocturnal and crepuscular bird of dry, rocky jungle and semi-open country with grasslands interspersed with orchards and tree plantations. Dark streaked overall, but belly unstreaked; sandy brown above and white below. Long bare legs with thickened knee joints. Large head and huge yellow eyes. A narrow, whitish bar and grey panel on closed wings. In flight, two narrow white bars and a white patch on the black primaries discernable, creating a very distinctive effect in the headlights. Feeds on small reptiles, insects, slugs; also seeds. Call a clear '*cur-lee*'.

Greater Thick-knee *Esacus magnirostris* 51cm

437

E Hanumantha Rao

Essentially a crepuscular and nocturnal bird of boulder-strewn riverbanks; occasionally near the sea. Sandy grey-brown above, with a thickset head and an enormous, upturned black and yellow beak. Large yellow eyes surrounded by white; with three black bands each above, below and behind it. A blackish band near shoulder of closed wing. A wash of grey on neck and breast, rest white. Duck-like profile in flight, with an arched back, and white patches on black primaries. Feeds on crabs. Sometimes seen basking on a rock beside water with the sun blazing overhead.

Indian Courser *Cursorius coromandelicus* 26cm   **440**

E Hanumantha Rao

A plover-like, long-legged bird of open country. Sandy-brown above with bright rufous crown; black eye-stripe and white supercilium extending to nape. Throat and breast chestnut. Upper abdomen black, undertail white. Legs long and pure white; wing quills black. Runs in spurts and stops, dipping and bending down to reach the ground to feed. When disturbed has the same running and stopping routine, stretching to take a look at the observer. Usually flies low over the ground, but when much harried, will fly high and fast, the pointed wings looking somewhat like a pratincole's.

Joanna Van Gruisen

The Small Pratincole is gregarious and can be found flycatching over placid rivers and associated wide banks, or near other large bodies of water. Brown and sandy-grey above, brown and white below. Tail coverts and tail white, but black at tip. A band from eye to bill black. Primaries black, contrasting with white base of secondaries and grey mantle in flight; also dark underwing contrasts with white underparts. Wings long and flight highly manoeuvrable, giving the general impression of swallows. Tends to be crepuscular.

G & H Denzau

A Jungle Crow-sized migratory gull of sea coast and large bodies of water. Mantle and back pale grey with white rump. Underparts white. Wing-tips black with a white spot or 'mirror' on the outer primaries. Head white with dark spot on ear coverts. When breeding has a brown face hood; doing so in Ladakh within the limits of the region. Red bill and legs. A gregarious scavenger, associating with kites and other gulls escorting boats and ships near harbours. Lands on water, floating buoyantly and high.

Otto Pfister

Smaller than the Brown-headed Gull, this species is about the size of the House Crow, and is migratory. Head, neck, rump, tail and underparts white. Small brown spots in front of eye and behind ear. Back and wings grey with the underside of primaries black. No 'mirrors' on wing, and black tip to red bill help separate it from the Brown-headed. Develops a dark brown face hood when breeding, which can be seen on some individuals before departure. Does not usually dive into water, but does settle on it, riding high and buoyantly. Feeds on offal, fish, prawns, insects, earthworms.

Whiskered Tern *Chlidonias hybrida* 25cm 458

Joanna Van Gruisen

A slim, almost square-tailed tern of both inland and coastal waters. When not breeding, silvery-grey above and white below, with a black eye-stripe extending on to the nape, and a grey crown having black flecks. When breeding, overall darker with black crown cap and grey-black underparts separated by pure white chin, throat and cheeks. Legs and beak red. Gregarious, in pairs or small flocks. Does not usually dive into the water, but tends to flick prey off the surface by dipping only the bill. Also catches flying insects.

A graceful bird of placid fresh waters, the River Tern is about the size of the House Crow and has a deeply forked tail, yellow beak and red legs. Deep grey of back and wings contrasts with light grey rump and off-white underparts. A black forehead-crown-nape cap when breeding; paler with white flecks when non-breeding; also blackish tip to bill in this period. In winter, black on crown and nape reduced to flecks. Utters an occasional harsh, screeching note. Dives by plunging into the water for fish; rests on rocks or sandbanks when full.

Indian Skimmer *Rynchops albicollis* 40cm   484

Found on placid waters of larger tanks and reservoirs, larger rivers, and inshore coastal waters and estuaries. Underparts and forehead white, upperparts black, the black of head and back separated by a white collar. Legs red, bill orange-yellow, yellowish at tip. In flight, upperwing black, underwing white; and a dark stripe down middle of white rump and tail. Has a laterally compressed, knife-like beak, the lower mandible of which is longer. This it dips into the water with the beak held open and flies skimming the water's surface. Any fish coming in contact with the lower mandible slides up the incline and the beak snaps shut catching the fish. Found singly or in loose flocks. Calls out in shrill screams.

Chestnut-bellied Sandgrouse *Pterocles exustus* 28cm 487

R K Gaur

A typical sandgrouse of the plains, avoiding forests, coastal thickets or hilly country. Greatly elongated central tail feathers and a black band across breast help to distinguish this species from other sandgrouse. Buff predominates as a colour in both the sexes, with the main flight feathers being much darker. Head and neck of male rather unpatterned, rest with speckles and banding; cheeks, chin and throat dull yellow, belly dark chocolate. Female has the upperparts streaked, spotted and barred with dark brown, as is the upper breast. Abdomen darker and closely barred with blackish.

Painted Sandgrouse *Pterocles indicus* 28cm   492

Foto Media

A pigeon-sized, dumpy bird of semi-arid tracts. A finely close-barred pattern dominates the plumage in both the sexes, with the crown and nape being streaked. Male has the forehead white and a broad black band on the fore-crown; also a tricoloured breast-band. Unpatterned throat and breast. Female lacks the fore-crown patterning and breast colours of the male. In this species, both sexes lack the pin-like central main tail feathers. Pairs or around half a dozen birds together, and larger groups at the end of the monsoon, coming regularly in the mornings and evenings to water holes, a characteristic habit.

Yellow-legged Green Pigeon *Treron phoenicoptera* 33cm 504

An arboreal, fruit-eating pigeon of groves, avenues and deciduous forests. Olive-green and ashy-grey above, bright yellow below. A lilac patch and yellow band on wing. The north Indian race has the abdomen and flanks grey. The yellow legs are diagnostic of the species. Sexes alike but female duller. Rather an inactive bird, collecting in numbers on fruit-laden fig trees. Moves about on the branches rather like a parakeet; being quite inconspicuous due to the obliterative colouring of the plumage. Tends to 'freeze' when disturbed, closely watching the observer from between leaves, with only an inadvertent movement disclosing its presence.

Eurasian Collared Dove *Streptopelia decaocto* 32cm 534

A dove of open country with trees, especially in the dry deciduous zone. Grey and brown above with a distinct, white-bordered, black half-collar on hind-neck. Breast lilac turning ashy-grey on belly. Tail feathers dark, but white terminally. Sexes alike. A common dove which can get quite trusting of humans. Found in pairs, which could grow into large aggregations in the non-breeding season where food is plentiful. Has a low, 'dreamy', three-noted call, and a more vehement version during aggression. Widespread throughout the country, more commonly in north-western, western and central India.

E Hanumantha Rao

A small, myna-sized dove of open scrub and cultivation. The smallest of the Indian doves, and also the only one where the sexes differ. Male's head is grey, mantle wine-red and lower back and tail brown. A black hind-collar, wine-red underparts which are whitish towards the chin and tail, and some grey under the wing present. Female is more or less like the female of the Eurasian Collared Dove, but distinctly smaller: brown above, greyish on head and rump, and with a light brown breast. A dark hind-collar. Both sexes have the tips of the outer tail feathers white. Shares the habitat with Eurasian Collared and Little Brown Doves, being rather uncommon on the whole.

Spotted Dove *Streptopelia chinensis* 30cm   537

Krupakar Senani

A familiar dove of gardens and parks, with a characteristic broad black collar on the hind-neck, boldly spotted with white. Upperparts brown spotted with pink; the head being grey. Tail dark, but white terminally; the white showing off as a flashy band when tail spread while alighting. White and grey underparts. Prefers moister conditions than either the Little Brown or Eurasian Collared Doves, being found in groves, cultivation and deciduous forests. Wanders about picking up seed and grain, fluttering off when flushed. A soft '*kroo-kroo-kroo*' call.

S Nagaraj

A small, slender dove of dry areas, stony scrubby country and cultivation. Earthy-brown above, with a lilac-pink head and neck, and grey patches on shoulders. Wing feathers darker. Broad, black collar on fore-neck boldly spotted with ferruginous. Underparts white and rufous, with greyish flanks and white tip to outer tail feathers. A typical dove, keeping in pairs or small groups, gleaning seeds and grain. Can become quite trusting of human presence, even building nests on rafters and in verandas. Has a soft, many-syllabled, cooing call; somewhat harsh but pleasant '*cru-do-do*'. Widespread throughout the country and up to 1200m in the outer Himalayas.

Emerald Dove *Chalcophaps indica* 27cm   542

Krupakar Senani

A small, forest-dwelling ground dove, only larger than a myna. Wings and back dark, shining green; tail black with white outer tail feathers. Head, neck and underparts grey, varying in tint on the various parts. A white bar on the shoulders; white forehead and supercilium. Beak coral-red; legs pink. Feeds on seeds, grain, fallen berries and fruits; in forest and plantation, also in secondary growth. Can be seen running about gleaning on forest trails and paths, or near cultivation clearings in forest. Flight is very swift and silent. Active in the mornings and evenings, and can be rather difficult to approach.

Alexandrine Parakeet *Psittacula eupatria* 51cm

This pigeon-sized bird is the largest of the parakeets inhabiting forest and woodland in both dry and moist deciduous zones. Overall grass-green, varying in tint on various parts, with the long, graduated tail being green, verditer blue and yellow. A large dark red patch near the wrist of the wing. The rose-pink collar on sides and back of the neck is completed in the front by a black band. Massive red bill, legs greyish or yellowish depending on race. Female and immatures lack the pink collar and black mandibular stripe. The shoulder patch, deeper calls, and more stately and slower flapping of wings in flight distinguish it from the familiar Rose-ringed Parakeet.

Rose-ringed Parakeet *Psittacula krameri* 42cm

The most common and abundant of the region's parakeets. A grass-green bird with the green varying in tint on the various parts, with the lower plumage more yellowish. A green tail turning yellow on the inner webs. Black chin extends as a short band to join the rose-pink collar going round sides and back of neck in male. Female has an indistinct emerald-green collar. Avoids heavy forest, but found in wooded areas, orchards, cultivation, also avenues, gardens and parks in towns and cities. Arboreal, but coming down to crop fields to feed on ears of grain. In the evenings, flock after flock fly to roost in the same path at tree-top level. A screeching, *'kree-kree'* call.

Relatively small and more slender than most other parakeets, preferring woodland and forest. Male has a yellowish-green plumage, plum-red head, black and bluish-green collar and maroon-red shoulder (wing) patch. The white tip to central tail feathers are distinctive. The female has a dull bluish-grey head, a yellow collar and an almost non-existent maroon shoulder patch. Found in pairs or small groups, sometimes in much larger gatherings. Has a pleasant '*tooi-tooi*' call, as well as other notes when perched. Feeds on fruit, grains, buds, fleshy petals and flower nectar. Flight direct and swift.

Slaty-headed Parakeet *Psittacula himalayana* 41cm   562

A grass-green parakeet of the Himalayan woodlands and neighbouring cultivation, which is about the size of the Rose-ringed. Head slaty-grey; a narrow black ring round the neck joins the black chin. A bright bluish-green hind-collar; tail blue and green tipped with bright yellow. Female differs from the male in having a dark red patch on secondary coverts. General habits like the Blossom-headed, with similar but distinguishable call. Only more individualistic, and not aggregating into such large flocks. Utters a high-pitched but pleasant, double-noted '*tooi-tooi*' call.

Pied Cuckoo *Clamator jacobinus* 33cm

A myna-sized cuckoo of lightly wooded country, gardens and groves. Black above and white below with the prominent crest also being black. The tail is long and graduated with white-tipped feathers. Sexes alike. Immatures are duller, with both the black and white being more brownish, and a less developed crest. Populations subject to a lot of little understood seasonal movements. Arboreal but coming down occasionally to feed on its insect food. Has a variety of calls, the more frequent being a loud, metallic '*piew-piew*'. Widespread in most of the country, south of outer Himalayas.

Common Hawk-Cuckoo *Cuculus varius* 34cm

A Shikra-like, pigeon-sized cuckoo of well-wooded areas, orchards, groves and gardens. Ashy-grey above and dull white anteriorly below, with pale ashy-rufous on breast; bars on lower breast and belly. The flight feathers are browner and in the closed wing, the primaries extend beyond the secondaries only by about a third or less of the total length from wrist to end of primaries: a character which distinguishes it from all other Indian cuckoos except the Large Hawk Cuckoo. Tail grey, tipped and barred four or five times with rufous. Eyes and legs yellow. Famous for its '*pipeetia*' call, repeated over and over.

Asian Koel *Eudynamys scolopacea* 43cm 590

Nikhil Devasar

The most common and the most widely known of the cuckoos in the region, being found only in lightly wooded country including parks and gardens. Sexes dimorphic. Male glistening black and very crow-like, but much slimmer, with green bill and crimson eyes. Female dark brown profusely barred and spotted with white all over. Arboreal, though individuals could come down to the ground for anting occasionally. The song of the male is a shrill, screaming '*kuoo-kuoo*' rising in scale, seven or more notes in sequence, but not rising in pitch after the seventh. A fruit eater, parasitic on crows.

Greater Coucal *Centropus sinensis* 48cm 600

Foto Media

A large, Jungle Crow-sized, unmistakable cuckoo of light forest, scrub and bush jungle, and manmade woodland habitats. Overall unpatterned black with chestnut wings. A broad, long, graduated tail. Iris crimson; bill and legs black. Sexes alike, but female slightly larger. Spends a lot of time on the ground, walking about and feeding on insects and small animals. Keeps singly or in pairs, skulking through the undergrowth, tending to fly low when disturbed. A distinctive '*coop-coop-coop*' call, quickly repeated, deep and resonant, unforgettable once heard.

Barn Owl *Tyto alba* 36cm

T Dalip Singh

A ghostly pale, medium-sized owl with a large, round head and a distinct 'facial disc'. Upperparts light golden orange-buff vermiculated with black and white. Underparts white with fine, dark brown spots. No aigrettes or ear tufts. With a worldwide distribution, the Barn Owl favours the vicinity of cultivation, woodland and human settlements, like ruins of old forts and buildings, and rocky areas. Nocturnal, but can be seen out in the day on rare occasions. Has an eerie, long-drawn shriek often uttered on the wing, various other chuckles, snoring and hissing sounds, the last especially when disturbed at the nest.

Eurasian Eagle Owl *Bubo bubo* 56cm

S Nagaraj

An inhabitant of vegetated hummocks, ravines, valleys and eroded lands. This owl is overall dark brown, streaked and mottled with buff and black. Eyes orangish, and fully feathered legs distinguish it from similar species. Has two aigrettes ('horns') on the head, held rather erect, in similar fashion to the Brown Fish Owl. Roosts by day in a rock fissure or in some densely canopied tree, flying off a good distance when disturbed. A deep, resonant, far-carrying '*bu-bo*' call, repeated at intervals. Feeds on rodents; also reptiles, frogs and medium-sized birds.

Spotted Owlet *Athene brama* 21cm

E Hanumantha Rao

The owl you are most likely to see in the region. Genus named after Pallas Athene, the Greek goddess of wisdom. This small owl has white spots on a grey-brown plumage and is seen in pairs or small groups. Flies to the next perch on being disturbed, turns round and bobs its head up and down in a most endearing fashion. Makes an assortment of screeching and scolding noises. Feeds on insects, small rodents, lizards and birds. Is found in open forests, orchards, farmland and even in villages and cities. Widespread throughout the country.

Mottled Wood Owl *Strix ocellata* 48cm

Nanda Rana

A large, beautiful owl of woodland and groves, variously patterned with spots, bars, streaks and bands giving a very mottled appearance. The plumage colours include reddish-brown, black and white. No aigrettes or ear tufts. Facial disk prominent, mottled and barred black and white bordered with a ruff. A whitish half-collar on neck; tail banded. Distinguished from other similar owls by the closely barred underparts, with no streaks or spots, and the very characteristic and distinct call: an eerie, long 'laugh', '*huhua-a-a-a-a*', easily remembered once heard.

Krupakar Senani

 A nightjar of scrub and deciduous forest, with a monotonous '*chuck-chuck*' call repeated at a rate of two to three chucks per second. Also a somewhat whistling '*chuckoo-chuckoo*' continued for many minutes and a pleasant '*uk ku kroo*', both repeated more slowly than the first call. A typical nightjar, the eyes large and bright, gleaming red on illumination; a wide beak, short legs, long wings, noiseless flight, and a soft ashy-brown plumage mottled darker. A buff 'V' on back. Hawks insects, after darkness has set in, over the canopy or closer to the ground in clearings and glades.

Large-tailed Nightjar *Caprimulgus macrurus* 33cm   675

T Dalip Singh

 A brownish-buff forest nightjar with a continuous loud and resonant '*chaunk-chaunk-chaunk*' call (also rendered '*chock-chock-chock*'). Vocal between dusk and dawn; calls help identification. Sexes alike but the female more rufous. The palest of the nightjars, coming out at sunset to hawk insects in the manner of a swallow, and perching both across and along a branch. Forages well above the canopy, and also in glades and clearings. Shares general habits with other nightjars. Settles down on forest roads and paths, avoiding oncoming vehicles in the nick of time. Widespread.

Joanna Van Gruisen

A kingfisher of Himalayan streams and confluences, the largest of the region, with wings and tail boldly barred and spotted with white. A prominent crest present. Distinctive; differs from Pied Kingfisher in having no supercilium, the white chin and throat separated from the white cheek patch by a thin, dark band joining the beak with the darker sides of neck. A black and rufous-brown breast-band; posterior ventral part and side barred with blackish. Female like male, but has underwing coverts and armpits reddish brown. Found in pairs and does not hover like its smaller relative. Uncommon and wary.

Joanna Van Gruisen

A speckled, myna-sized, black and white kingfisher with a small black crest. The female differs from the male in having a single breast-band broken in the middle, while the male's is double and complete. A prominent white supercilium, and an indistinct white collar on hind-neck. A plains bird always found near water, the Pied Kingfisher has a fantastic hover while fishing. Flies over the water some five metres above the surface, stopping suddenly in a hover with a slight increase in height, bill pointing down as if intently taking aim. Plunges headlong into water.

E Hanumantha Rao

A small green, blue and rust-coloured kingfisher, a little larger than a sparrow in size. Top of head very finely barred with black and blue. A ferruginous ear-stripe ending in a white patch on the side of neck and a low, blue cheek stripe. Lores and bill black, chin and throat white, legs coral-red, underparts bright rust. Found singly or in pairs perched on a stake or rock adjoining water. Has a habit of bobbing its head up and down when perched. Flies low over water when disturbed. A shrill, not unpleasant, '*chichichee*' call, uttered when darting over water.

Oriental Dwarf Kingfisher *Ceyx erithacus* 13cm 727

Joanna Van Gruisen

A tiny kingfisher, perhaps the most beautiful in the region, this species is found in deep evergreen and moist deciduous forests. Bright coral-red legs and feet, orange-rufous head and neck with violet-blue and white patch; orange-yellow underparts with white chin and throat. Lilac mantle with blue streak down back. Dark wings. Catches small fish, crustaceans and the like from shaded forest streams; also picks off insects from the forest floor. Other general habits like that of Common: including the darting off on approach. Has a sharp, squeaky '*chicheee*' call.

Stork-billed Kingfisher *Pelargopsis capensis* 38cm 730

Joanna Van Gruisen

A huge kingfisher of placid waters in wooded habitats. A greyish-brown cap, a large, fat blood-red bill, a yellowish collar, and pale greenish-blue upperparts, along with white and brownish-yellow underparts, distinguish it from other kingfishers. Sexes alike. Rather secretive, perched hidden in the foliage overhanging water, darting down to capture any animal of manageable size. Feeds on fish, frogs and small birds. Has a loud noisy '*ke-ke-ke-ke-ke*' call, uttered when perched. Found single or in separated pairs. Widespread, all over the Indian region except drier parts of North-west.

White-throated Kingfisher *Halcyon smyrnensis* 28cm 736

Vivek Sinha

The least dependent on water amongst all the kingfishers, this species can even be found in wooded and parkland habitats. Turquoise-blue above, chocolate-brown below, on the head and neck. Coral-red bill. A white 'front' ventrally and a white wing patch conspicuous when flying. Spends a lot of time on the lookout for both swimming and crawling prey, up on a post or branch, flying out to pick up the hapless victim roller-like, which, if large, is battered before being gulped down. Feeds also on insects, frogs, lizards and occasionally on fish. A light, drawn-out 'laugh' for a call.

Kamal Sahai

A little larger than the myna in size, the Black-capped Kingfisher is essentially a saltwater species. A white collar separates the black cap from the deep blue upperparts. It is dull rufous ventrally, except for the throat and breast which are white. A white wing patch seen in flight and a typical coral-red kingfisher beak. Sexes alike. Call resembles that of the more common White-breasted Kingfisher but is easily distinguished once heard. Found chiefly on coastal areas, mangroves, estuaries; may wander inland, especially along rivers. Distributed all along the peninsular coast.

Chestnut-headed Bee-eater *Merops leschenaulti* 21cm   744

Krupakar Senani

One of the more beautiful bee-eaters of the region, this species has a yellow throat separated from the green underparts by a dark chestnut band; head, neck and back chestnut; wings and tail dark green. Uppertail coverts pale blue. Central tail feathers not extended with the tail appearing squarish. Sexes alike. Is gregarious like other bee-eaters, roosting communally. Found in forested and wooded tracts near streams and water courses. Feeds chiefly on winged insects, captured in flight. Likely to turn up in any appropriate habitat other than in its Western Ghat and Himalayan range, especially during the rains.

Green Bee-eater *Merops orientalis* 21cm 750

S Nagaraj

A common sparrow-sized bee-eater of open country, the smallest that we have in the family. Overall green, tinged with blue in places, especially on the throat. The head has some reddish-brown, and the brighter throat is bordered with a black gorget. A long, black, down-curved beak, central tail feather greatly elongated, though some individuals show no elongated pin feathers at times. In habits, typifies the bee-eater, gregarious, roosting communally in some leafy tree; and flycatching by sallying from electric poles, wires and such-like exposed perches in open country and cultivation.

Blue-bearded Bee-eater *Nyctyornis athertoni* 36cm 753

Joanna Van Gruisen

A large, about pigeon-sized bee-eater of degraded and opened-up evergreen and moist deciduous forest. Overall bright green and blue, the shades of green varying: head and neck tinged with verditer blue, the forehead being verditer blue; underparts shaded with buff, with the vent being buff. Undertail ochraceous-yellow, and elongate feathers of neck and breast deep blue. Beak is shorter and thicker than in other bee-eaters. Sexes alike. Croaking sound, often followed by softer chuckling call. A shy and rather inactive bird, usually keeping to the treetops. Flight undulating. Makes a harsh '*korrr-korrr*'.

Indian Roller *Coracias benghalensis* 31cm

Otto Pfister

A colourful bird of cultivation and open country found perched on some high vantage point on the lookout for insects on the ground. Pale greenish-brown above, with blue wings and tail, the flight feathers being deep purplish-blue with a prominent band of pale blue. Top of head bluish-green. Underparts both brownish and bluish. Not so conspicuous in the landscape, in flight the bird is transformed into a flashing bundle of light and dark blue, green and brown. Gets its name from the courtship display. Feeds mostly on lizards, frogs, small rodents and snakes.

Common Hoopoe *Upupa epops* 31cm

S Nagaraj

A fawn-coloured species with bold black and white banding on back, wings and tail. A fan-shaped, sagittal black-tipped crest, folding over the back of the head when not erected. Long slender bill with a shallow down-curve. Sexes alike. Feeds on grubs, pupae and adult insects. Has a deep but soft '*hoo-po*' or '*hoo-po-po*' call repeated over and over, whence the bird gets its name. Widespread, throughout the country, from about 5500m in Himalayas. Moves considerably in winter.

Indian Grey Hornbill *Tockus birostris* 61cm

Toby Sinclair

One of the smallest of the region's hornbills, but still kite-sized! Overall grey-brown, southern birds being more brown, with a small casque on bill, and black and white-tipped graduated tail. Female's casque is smaller. Arboreal, keeping in small groups, feeding on figs, other fruits, flower nectar, large insects and small animals. Flies from tree to tree in almost follow-the-leader fashion, and has an undulating flight. At times will come on to the ground to feed on fallen fruit and winged termite alates. Widespread, almost throughout India, from about 1500m in Himalayas. Absent in arid north-western regions and the heavy rainfall areas of southern Western Ghats.

Great Hornbill *Buceros bicornis* 130cm

Joanna Van Gruisen

The largest hornbill in the region, keeping to the wet and moist forests of Western Ghats, Himalayas and the north-east. This vulture-sized, endangered species has the huge bill and casque yellow, the latter ending in forked tip anteriorly. Tail white with a broad black band more towards the end, white neck and wing patches. Face and upperparts black. Female slightly smaller, with the posterior end of the casque red. Iris of male blood red and that of female white. Keeps together in small groups, flying from tree to tree in almost follow-the-leader formation, the birds maintaining a rigid punctuality in moving about in their home range.

Great Barbet *Megalaima virens* 33cm

The largest of the region's barbets, this bird is an inhabitant of the temperate moist forest of the Himalayas. Has a blackish head, brownish olive back and shoulders, the upperback streaked with yellow; wings and tail with green and blue, and prominent yellow beak. Ventrally, the upperbreast is dark olive-brown, the belly is striped yellow and brown with a blue median band. Vent is conspicuously scarlet and the undertail blackish. Keeps to the canopy of tall trees, unless coming down to the shrubbery to feed on fruit. Flight undulating and rather like a woodpecker's. Call is a far-carrying, loud, plaintive *'mee-ou'* repeated continuously in the breeding season.

Brown-headed Barbet *Megalaima zeylanica* 27cm

A grass-green barbet with the brownish head, neck, and upper back streaked with white. A large, bare, orange patch around the eyes extending to the beak. No white cheek stripe. Sexes alike. Entirely arboreal, only coming down to the shrubs to feed on fruit. Easily determined whether in an area by its loud, monotonous, far-carrying *'kutur-kutur'* call repeated incessantly in the breeding season. A hole-nesting species of forests, well-wooded areas and gardens with trees. Feeds chiefly on fruits; also flower nectar, petals, insects and small lizards.

Blue-throated Barbet *Megalaima asiatica* 23cm   788

M S Oberoi

A myna-sized bird of light forest and well-wooded country of the north. Overall grass-green, with a pale blue face, and crimson crown. The crimson hind-neck is enclosed within a black band going all round it, which is in turn bordered with yellow at the front. A large, crimson spot on each side of the neck. Remiges blackish, underparts yellower. Shares general habits with other barbets: arboreal and frugivorous, a dumpy appearance, undulating flight; and of course the typical monotonous call, three-syllabled in this species, which goes '*kutooruk-kutooruk*' for long stretches.

Coppersmith Barbet *Megalaima haemacephala* 17cm   792

E Hanumantha Rao

A dumpy, sparrow-sized, arboreal bird with a monotonous '*tuk-tuk*' call. A colourful species with red on the head and breast; yellow on the chin, throat and around the eye. A black eye mask. Upperparts green, and underparts streaked green on a yellow background. The calls are one of the best known in India and are likened to a coppersmith working on his metal. Nests in self-made holes and feeds on berries, figs and other fruits. Found in areas with trees, from village avenues and groves to urban parkland and gardens. Widespread throughout India from about 1800m in outer Himalayas.

Streak-throated Woodpecker *Picus myrmecophoneus* 29cm 808

A little larger than a myna in size, this woodpecker is grass-green with a yellow rump above, and greenish with a grey chin and throat below. Has white supercilium and malar stripe, the former bordered withblack. Underparts and flight feathers heavily patterned: the former scalloped and the latter banded and spotted. Male has a red crown and the female has it black. In addition to the typical woodpecker habit of chiselling the bark of trees for wood-boring insects, comes down to the ground to feed on ants and termites.

Black-rumped Flameback *Dinopiumbenghalense* 29cm 819

A black, white and golden-yellow woodpecker of groves, avenues and lightly wooded country. Crest crimson; the crown being crimson in the male and black in the female. Mantle golden-yellow; hind neck, lower back and tail black; sides of head and neck white. Underparts white, the black and white striped pattern of chin and throat gradually fading towards the posterior end. Usually found in pairs, working up the branches and trunks from a lower level, chipping away rotten wood and bark to feed on wood-boring insects, and ants. Seen all over India, from about 1800m in outer Himalayas.

89

A myna-sized wood-pecker of the cold, high Himalayan forests. Crown and crest crimson in male, black in female. Back black, with a prominent white elongated patch on shoulders, and white spots and bars on wing quills. A white cheek and ear covert patch bordered with black. Yellowish-brown below, extending up as a band at the base of the neck, varying in shade on the different parts. Vent and undertail crimson. Shares general habits with some other woodpeckers and in addition, in common with other Himalayan woodpeckers, drills small holes in rings around stems of trees.

Yellow-crowned Woodpecker
Picoides mahrattensis 18cm   847

A small woodpecker, smaller than a bulbul in size, found in lightly wooded country patchily throughout the region. Upperparts brownish-black heavily spotted with white. Forehead and crown yellow; crest scarlet in male, yellow in female. Underparts whitish anteriorly, the pale brown stripes of breast becoming darker and bolder posteriorly and ending in a scarlet patch. A deep red iris. Found individually in the non-breeding season, otherwise in pairs, in groves, avenues, scrub and gardens. Rather quiet and not attention-drawing. Widespread, commonly seen throughout India.

Grey-capped Pygmy Woodpecker *Picoides canicapillus* 14cm 849

Krupakar Senani

A tiny woodpecker, smaller than a sparrow, of Himalayan open and secondary forests. Upperparts black, boldly barred with white; forehead and crown ashy-grey, crest scarlet surrounded by black in male, all black in female. White sides of neck extend as a broad whitish supercilium. Partial to thin twigs, branches and stems, either high in the canopy or low near the ground, which are not used by other larger woodpeckers. A frequent member of mixed-species insectivorous flocks. An out-and-out woodpecker, albeit small!

Indian Pitta *Pitta brachyura* 19cm   867

S Karthikeyan

A many-coloured bird with short tail and legs, which feeds on the ground but takes shelter in bushes and trees when alarmed. Back and shoulders dull bluish-green, with a patch of pale blue feathers above the tail and in the wing. Eyebrows, chin and throat white. Head and breast orange-yellow; vent crimson. Crown and eye-stripe black. Sexes alike. Generally silent, keeping not far from cover, and silently flying up into a tree when disturbed, only to resume its activities after the danger has passed. Tends to come into lighted-up homes in the suburbs at night during migration.

Crested Lark *Galerida cristata* 18cm 899

Nikhil Devasar

A large lark, sandy-brown overall, but paler below, with prominent sharp crest raising upward and backward from the head. The bird is streaked with black above and brown below. There is no white in the tail. Seen in small flocks, breaking into pairs when breeding. Runs briskly on ground, the pointed crest carried upstanding. Settles on bush-tops, stumps, wire-fences and overhead wires. Feeds on seeds, grain, insects. Inhabits semi-desert, cultivation and dry grasslands. Found in North India, north-western India, Gangetic plain, south to Rajasthan, Saurashtra.

Oriental Skylark *Alauda gulgula* 16cm 907

Otto Pfister

A bird of open country, especially moist grasslands. Brown above, with dark streaks and paler scalloping. Tawny buff below, darker on breast, streaked and spotted with blackish. Slightly elongated feathers on crown, tending towards a crest, more visible when feathers fluffed or raised. No rufous on wing. Keeps in pairs or small parties, foraging on ground for insects, running about in spurts. Not inclined to perch on bushes or trees like bushlarks, squatting on ground when disturbed, and almost flushing from under one's foot. Display and song typical of the larks.

Joanna Van Gruisen

One of the prettier swallows in the Indian Subcontinent. Pure white of the underparts contrasts strongly with the glistening deep purplish-blue of the upperparts. The shafts of the two outer tail feathers project a good 10cm beyond rest of the tail; this is shorter in the female and absent in the young (and when in moult too). The young is brown, showing blue in patches. Habits and habitats similar to other swallows, but prefers neighbourhood of water. A resident species, roosting with wagtails and other swallows in reeds standing in water.

Great Grey Shrike *Lanius excubitor* 25cm   933

E Hanumantha Rao

The largest of the region's shrikes, the Great Grey Shrike is bluish-grey above, with broad, black eyestripe from beak through eyes. Black wings with white mirrors. White underparts, with outer feathers of black tail also white. A bird of open country, semi-desert and cultivation. Shares general habits with other shrikes, like impaling surplus prey on thorns, the prey being obtained by being picked off the ground or other substrata, after being located from a lookout perch. Call a harsh grating '*khreck*'; also a mix of other harsh notes and chuckles. Seen in the drier areas of north-western, west and central India.

Bay-backed Shrike *Lanius vittatus* 18cm 940

A small, pretty shrike, with deep chestnut-maroon back, black forehead extending as a broad eye-band beyond the ear coverts. Crown and hind-neck grey. White underparts with white patch on black wings, and white outer feathers in black tail. White on rump distinctive. Breast and flanks washed with reddish-brown. Sexes alike. Prefers less dry areas than the Great Grey Shrike; hanging around the same place day after day. Feeds on insects, lizards and small rodents. Found in open country, light forests and scrub, it is a resident species, but subject to seasonal movements. General habits like other shrikes.

Long-tailed Shrike *Lanius schach* 25cm 946

Intermediate in size between Great Grey and Bay-backed Shrikes, this species prefers the most moist conditions amongst the three. Overall bright rufous, paler below. Wings and central tail black. Head grey or black depending on the race. Has the black eye-stripe much narrower than the Bay-backed, especially at the forehead. Noisy. Voice a harsh rise. Prefers open areas with trees, forest edges and such-like habitats. Sexes alike. Shares the white patch on wing and general habits with other shrikes. Mostly solitary; boldly defends feeding territory.

Eurasian Golden Oriole *Oriolus oriolus* 25cm

Otto Pfister

This species is one of the few migrant frugivores in the region. The male is bright golden-yellow with a black stripe through the eye, black wings and tail. The female is yellowish-green above, dirty white streaked with brown below, and has brownish-green wings. Young male very much like the female. Arboreal, solitary or in pairs, feeding on fruit, flower nectar, caterpillars and other insects. Has a mellow fluid '*pe-lo-lo*' call and a harsh '*cheeah*'. The black of the eyestripe stopping just behind the eye distinguishes them from the rarer and the similar Black-naped Oriole. Found all over India in winter, breeding in the north.

Black-hooded Oriole *Oriolus xanthomas* 128cm

Krupakar Senani

A resident oriole of the moist tracts. Sexes largely alike. Overall golden-yellow with black head, black wing flight feathers and central tail; deep reddish-pink beak; legs darkish. Young have much less black on head and body, but breast is streaked with black. Habits similar to that of the more familiar Eurasian Golden Oriole. Call a nasal '*kwaak*', a harsh '*cheeah*', or melodious fluty whistles rendered as '*ru-yow-yow*' or '*tu-yow*'. Usually in pairs or small parties, keeping to trees. Associates itself with other birds in mixed parties, and is active.

Black Drongo *Dicrurus adsimilis* 31cm

963

Famed for its boldness, not even hesitating to attack a much larger crow in defending its nest, this is an all-black, glossy bird of cultivation and open country. Bulbul-sized, with deeply forked tail and deep red eyes. Uses exposed perches like tops of shrubs, scattered trees, electric wires and poles, as lookout posts from which to make sallies after flying insects. Similar migrant Grey Drongo of woodlands and forests has unglossed underparts, and the White-bellied Drongo of scrub has white belly. Widespread, most of India, up to about 1800m in outer Himalayas.

Greater Racket-tailed Drongo *Dicrurus paradiseus* 35cm   977

A large drongo of deciduous and ever-green forests. All black with unique tail and a crest of backwardly bent feathers. Intermediate por-tion of the long shafts of outer tail feathers bare, with an expanded racquet-like vane at the tip. Excellent mimic; has a variety of screams, whistles and perfect imita-tions of over a dozen species. Shares the habits of the group in making sallying flights to catch insects. Perhaps spends more time on the wing than its relatives. Also takes flower nectar, being easily attracted to such blooms that provide it.

Chestnut-tailed Starling *Sturnus malabaricus* 21cm 987

Krupakar Senani

A small, sociable member of the starling group. Upperparts dark grey with a reddish tinge, head pale grey; underparts rusty-red with throat and breast reddish-grey. Beak dark with yellow tip. The Western Ghat race *blythii* has the head and breast white. Arboreal, coming down to feed on fruits, insects and flower nectar in bushes, and very occasionally on to the ground. Like many other birds, attracted to emerging termites, and to trees in bloom that provide nectar. Aggregate into large groups by themselves or in association with other species of the family. Subject to seasonal movements.

Brahminy Starling *Sturnus pagodarum* 22cm 994

E Hanumantha Rao

A crested myna, but without any white spot on the wing, just as in the other members of this genus. Rich buff overall; with glossy black forehead, crown, nape and crest, the last lying flat on the neck somewhat like overgrown hair. Back grey; wings black and grey. Keeps together in small groups, forming larger associations at roosts and sites where food is available. Mixes freely with other mynas, feeding on fruit, flower nectar and large insects. Has a variety of not unpleasant calls, mixed with mimicked calls of other birds. The Brahminy Starling is subject to seasonal movements.

 A fast-flying migratory starling of open areas. Overall characteristic rose-pink with black head, neck, upperbreast, wings and tail. A long, pointed crest on crown and nape, raised partially when excited. Sexes alike. Immatures have the pink of the adult replaced by a pinkish-grey or a pale coffee, with the crest less prominent. Inhabits cultivation, grassland and low thorn jungle, coming into towns and cities occasionally. Feeds on grain, insects and flower nectar. Very noisy; voice a mix of guttural screams, chattering sounds and melodious whistles. A winter visitor to India. Widespread.

Common Starling *Sturnus vulgaris* 20cm 997

 A migratory bird visiting the north. Glossy black, with small yellow or buff spotting, sometimes showing a green or a bronze sheen. Highly gregarious; of ten in attendance on cattle and sheep, running behind them to grab fleeing insects. Shares the habit with some others of the genus in that a feeding flock, for no apparent reason, suddenly takes to the air en masse, to resume feeding later. Roosts communally in dense canopied trees, as with others of the group. Voice a mix of squeaking, clicking notes. Common in parts of northern India in winter. Feeds on insects, berries, earthworms and small lizards.

Asian Pied Starling *Sturnus contra* 23cm 1002

A distinct-looking myna with a pied plumage, orangish-red beak and orbital skin. Upperparts and wing black, with white rump; underparts white with black chin and throat. A white patch behind eye. Sociable in the non-breeding season, forming small flocks. General habits like other sturnids, spending a lot of time on the ground. Less trusting of humans than other mynas; also less fond of flower nectar, preferring more insect food. Unlike other mynas, is not a hole-nester, building untidy domed or globular nests placed high up in trees.

Common Myna *Acridotheres tristis* 23cm 1006

The most common of our mynas, occurring in a variety of habitats and wherever human habitations are present. Overall rich wine-brown, with black head, neck and upper breast. Yellow beak, legs and bare patch around eye. Large white patch on dark brown flight feathers characteristic of genus. Takes a variety of food: kitchen scraps, fruits, flower nectar, large insects like grasshoppers, geckos and small lizards. A hole-nester, roosting in large aggregations often along with House and Jungle Crows, often traditionally for many decades, in dense-canopied trees, many a time in roadside avenues.

Bank Myna *Acridotheres ginginianus* 21cm 1008

E Hanumantha Rao

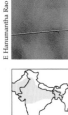

A gregarious resident myna of central and northern India which keeps together in flocks even during its breeding season. Like the Indian Myna, but with a short tuft on the forehead and overall plumage being grey instead of brown. Bare patch around eye dull red instead of yellow. Again, like the Indian Myna, a bird of a variety of habitats, from bazaars of towns and cities to complete outskirts of villages. Takes a variety of food, fruits, grain, grubs and insects, ticks picked off cattle, and eatables flicked from hand cart vendors! Other habits as in the group.

Hill Myna *Gracula religiosa* 29cm 1015

Krupakar Senani

A famed talker, but a noisy bird of the forest, keeping mostly to the canopy of moist, deciduous and evergreen forests. A jet-black myna with bright orange-yellow beak, pale yellow legs, yellow facial skin and fleshy wattles on nape and sides of face. A white wing bar. Larger than the common mynas; in small flocks or pairs, occasionally aggregating in large numbers on fruit-laden trees. Hardly ever comes to the ground, but does very rarely come down to the shrubbery. Towards sunset, moves on to the tall trees that tower over the high canopy of the rainforest, calling and screeching, before moving to the roost for the night.

Yellow-billed Blue Magpie *Cissa flavirostris* 66cm 1025

Joanna Van Gruisen

A pigeon-sized bird of the Himalayan wet temperate, mixed conifer and broad-leaved forest. A beautiful bird with long, graduated tail and streamers. Upperparts and nape patch white; head, neck, and breast black; rest of the body an eye-catching purplish-blue. Bill, legs and feet orange-yellow. Gregarious in the non-breeding season, keeping together in small flocks. Mainly tree-dwelling but does come down to shrubs and ground. Takes a variety of food: fruits, insects and other animal matter, also grain. A bird with a good vocabulary, many a time mimicking other species.

Red-billed Blue Magpie *Cissa erythrorhyncha* 70cm 1027

Joanna Van Gruisen

Rather similar to the Yellow-billed Blue Magpie in plumage and habits. Pigeon-sized with the head, neck and breast black, a long, graduated tail with extended streamers and off-white underparts. White patch on nape and hind-neck larger than in Yellow-billed. Bill, legs and feet red. Sexes alike. Shares habits and habitats with the Yellow-billed species, but tends to prefer lower elevations. Also tends to be more confiding, making its appearance at the Himalayan hill stations more often. Noisy; call a mix of metallic screams, loud whistles and raucous notes.

Rufous Treepie *Dendrocitta vagabunda* 50cm 1032

S Nagaraj

A not-so-shy, magpie-like bird of jungle, plantation and garden. Overall rufous, with grey head, neck and breast. Long, broad tail. A catholic feeder, taking fruit, small vertebrates, nestlings, eggs, carrion, a variety of insects, spiders, snails, and flower nectar. More often than not, keeps to the trees, associates with other species on fruit-laden trees, or at sites where insects are swarming. Flight direct; usually first glimpsed when flying from tree to tree, preferring the thicker foliage to get in. Has a variety of harsh and pleasant calls, one of the latter being an oriole-like '*bob-o-link*'.

Red-billed Chough *Pyrrhocorax pyrrhocorax* 45cm 1046

Joanna Van Gruisen

A House Crow-sized, all-black bird with bright red legs and red, slender, slightly curved beak. Found in high mountainous areas, with cliffs, alpine meadows, barren rocks or cultivation. Trusts man, roosts in man-made structures, rock fissures and caves. Gregarious, forms large flocks of over a hundred birds sometimes, feeds on grubs, other insects, barley. Has a musical plaintive call, and other notes as well. Not given to as much scavenging as the other members of the genus. Seen in high Himalayas, 2200-400m; may descend to about 1500m in severe winter.

Joanna Van Gruisen

Hardly merits a description since it is so common, ubiquitous, and distinctive. Overall black with grey neck, mantle and breast, with the face also being black. Present wherever human presence is there. Alert and adaptive, and predominantly a scavenger. Opportunistic and quick to grab a morsel of food when situations permit. Bold at such activities, but also generally wary, avoiding potentially dangerous situations. Though not as aggressive and daring as its larger relative, the Jungle Crow, will not hesitate to mob and attack predators. Roosts communally in large numbers, at sites which tend to be traditional.

Large-billed Crow *Corvus macrorhynchos* 48cm   1057

Joanna Van Gruisen

An all-black crow, larger in size than the common House Crow. Plumage shiny and iridescent, the shades varying between races and regions. An aggressive and daring species, does not hesitate to attack larger animals and predators for either robbing food or in defence of the young. Diet variable; will eat almost anything man would, and something more! Roosts communally with other crows and mynas at sites that tend to be traditional, with the same tree and same area being colonised for decades. Territorial and aggressive. Groups collect to 'mourn' fellow brethren who have died. Produces a variety of gurgling croaks.

Common Wood Shrike *Tephrodornis pondkerianus* 16cm 1070

An arboreal, generally quiet, ashy-brown bird with pale supercilium and a dark eye-band. Outer tail feathers white, noticeable in flight. The eye-band could be paler in the female. Found in open forests, gardens away from habitation, and the like. Searches foliage for insects, hopping about on the branches. Keeps together in small parties or in pairs. Builds a cup nest in a tree fork. Widespread, throughout the region, south of Himalayan foothills; commoner in low country. Feeds on insects and flower nectar. A whistling '*wheet-wheet*' followed by an interrogative, quick-repeated '*whi-whi-whee*' call thereafter.

Scarlet Minivet *Pericrocotus flammeus* 20cm 1081

A flock of Scarlet Minivets illuminated by the rich red of the setting sun over the forest canopy is indeed a spectacular sight. Male bright orange to scarlet (southern race orange) and black; female and immatures grey, bright yellow and black. In the male, the head and shoulders, wings and median tail feathers are black, while in the female, only the wings and median tail feathers are black, the head and back being grey. The wing has two wing bars, running along, not across as is usual in a closed wing, orange-scarlet or yellow, depending on the sex. Keeps to trees in forested tracts.

104

Small Minivet *Pericrocotus cinnamomeus* 15cm

Smaller and less colourful than the Scarlet Minivet, this species is found in more open country. The male has dark grey upperparts with wings and tail being black. The flame-orange breast fades to white at the belly. Orange-yellow patch on the wings. Female overall paler with the red replaced by yellow. Habits similar to the rest of the group. Pairs or small flocks keep to treetops, fluttering and flitting amidst foliage in an untiring hunt for insects, sometimes catching them in the air. Often in association with other small birds. Found in open forests, parks, gardens and tree-dotted cultivation.

Common Iora *Aegithina tiphia* 14cm 1098

Quite often given away by its rich, whistling, interrogative *'whe-eee-eeu?'* or similar call much earlier than it is seen, the Iora is a common bird of scrub and woodland, parks and gardens. The male is a trim black and yellow, with two white wing bars. Female is yellowish-green, also with the same wing bars. Non-breeding male is like female but with black tail. Keeps to the upper layers of the vegetation, behaving tit-like, perching in all positions to peer beneath leaves and twigs, and hopping from twig to twig in its forays for insects and their larvae. Widespread, throughout the country. Absent in arid north-west.

Golden-fronted Leafbird *Chloropsis aurifrons* 19cm   1103

Vivek Sinha

A bird of well-wooded areas, the overall camouflaging leaf-green makes it more easily heard than spotted. Often seen when flying from the canopy of one tree to another. Golden-orange forehead, blue shoulder patches, dark blue chin and throat (tending to be dark in the south) and a black border to the blue of the throat, characteristic. Female duller, with smaller orange patch on forehead. An excellent mimic of other birds, often putting to serious test one's capabilities to recognise calls. A canopy species feeding on fruit, nectar and insects, and a frequent member of the mixed 'hunting' flocks of the wet forests.

Asian Fairy Bluebird *Irena puella* 27cm   1109

Asad Rahmani

Named after the Greek goddess of peace, Eirene, and 'puella' meaning a maiden, thus suggesting something pretty, the Asian Fairy Bluebird is indeed a very beautiful bird. A brilliant, shimmering deep blue above and velvety black below, the male is one of the most striking birds of the wet forests of the eastern Himalayas and the Western Ghats. The female is more plain, being dull greenish-blue with dark lores. Found in canopy of trees, feeding on fruits and nectar in small groups or pairs, sometimes coming lower down into the understory. Has a rich and mellow '*peepyt*' call, uttered frequently.

Red-whiskered Bulbul *Pycnonotus jocosus* 20cm   1120

Krupakar Senani

Along with the Red-vented, the most common of the region's bulbuls. Brown above and white below, with a pointed black crest, red patches on the cheeks (whiskers) and red vent. The race in the Western Ghats has the pectoral band almost unbroken. Sexes alike. Lively and energetic, enlivening their surroundings with their cheerful, liquid (almost yodelling) notes. Its more musical calls are readily distinguishable from the Red-vented's. Takes fruits, nectar and insects; in gardens, jungles and parks. Tame and confiding in some areas. Seen from Garhwal east along Himalayan foothills to about 1500m; more common south of Satpura mountains in peninsular India.

White-eared Bulbul *Pycnonotus leucogenys* 20cm   1125

S Nagaraj

Essentially a northern Indian species, this bulbul too, like the others, adds a lot of cheer to its surroundings by its lively calls. Brown above with a black crest (varying in shape and extent in different zones) and white underparts. This species differs from the Red-whiskered and the Red-vented Bulbuls in having white cheeks, and yellow under the tail (vent). Found in drier areas than the other bulbuls in this book. Takes berries and other fruits, insects and flower nectar. Like the Red-whiskered, can become quite tame and trusting in areas. Seen in pairs or small parties, this Himalayan bird is common in Kashmir.

107

Red-vented Bulbul *Pycnonotus cafer* 20cm   1128

Otto Pfister

The Red-vented Bulbul is, like its close relative the Red-whiskered, a lively bird with cheerful calls. The upperparts and breast are brown with a blunt black crest, red vent and white rump, the last noticeable in flight. Differs from the Red-whiskered Bulbul in the shape of its crest, in having no red on the cheeks and in the colour of the breast. The call is also shorter with a syllable less. Shares the general habits with other bulbuls. Found in drier areas than Red-whiskered, like scrubland, and gardens. Feeds on insects, fruits, flower nectar and kitchen scraps. Widespread, throughout the country.

Black Bulbul *Hypsipetes madagascariensis* 23cm   1148

Krupakar Senani

A large bulbul of the hills, this species is essentially a bird of the forest and jungle. It is overall dull black with a prominent crest, distinctly forked tail, red beak and legs. Sexes alike. Generally keeps to the canopy and upper layers of the vegetation. Gregarious, moving about in small flocks which can grow into large aggregations on occasion. Has an assortment of harsh, screeching and whistling calls; quite noisy. Takes fruit, flower nectar and insects, the last sometimes in the manner of a flycatcher. Found in tall forests and hill station gardens.

Yellow-eyed Babbler *Chrysomma sinense* 18cm 1231

Vivek Sinha

A somewhat shy babbler of scrub and grassland, found in small groups gleaning insects and their larvae in the low growth, but not inclined to get down on to the ground. Upperparts fulvous-brown, turning cinnamon on the exposed portions of the closed wing. White patch near eye continues with the white underparts. Deeply graduated tail faintly cross-rayed. Iris yellow, with the eye-ring deep orange. Shares the habit with wren-warblers of taking a break in the hunt for food, clambering up stems to the sunlit portion, sunning itself with a snatch of singing, only to resume the gleaning for food immediately.

Common Babbler *Turdoides caudatus* 23cm 1254

Otto Pfister

A prominently streaked babbler with a long graduated tail. Overall fulvous-brown, with each feather streaked darker, and with the outer web paler. Underparts also paler, with the belly creamy-buff. Bill and legs yellow-brown. Crown with dark streaks, and an unstreaked whitish throat noticeable. Sexes alike. A bird of dry habitats, only occasionally entering cultivation and gardens. Noisy; pleasant, warbling whistles in squeaky alarm-notes. Commonly seen in most of north-western, western and peninsular India. Feeds on insects, berries and flower nectar.

Large Grey Babbler *Turdoides malcolmi* 28cm

The largest babbler of the genus in the region; with a characteristic '*kay-kay-kay*' call, and a brief alarm note. Forehead ashy-grey with fine shaft stripes, rest of upper plumage fulvous-brown, the feathers of the upper plumage having darker centres. Median tail feathers faintly cross-rayed, with the outer tail feathers white, prominent in flight. Lower plumage pale fulvous, darker on chin and breast. Noisy and gregarious, feeding on ground and on low trees; quite alert. Found in open country, scrub jungle, periphery of forestry plantations in dry areas, cultivation, village environs and campuses.

Jungle Babbler *Turdoides striatus* 25cm

An earthy-brown species which moves about in small flocks, rummaging through leaves in search of food. The underparts are paler, with the long broad tail (a big tail!) faintly cross-hatched. Has pale-yellowish eyes, yellowish bill and legs. A resident species found in scrub, cultivation, village and town outskirts with trees; and in open forest. Gregarious with flocking continuing even during breeding; spends a lot of time on the ground, hopping and maintaining a lively chatter, but flying into trees when disturbed. Has a harsh '*ke-ke-ke*' call, along with other loud and soft 'conversation' maintained in the flock.

White-throated Laughing Thrush *Garrulax albogularis* 28cm 1274

R K Gaur

Found in the high- and medium-altitude, heavy forests of the Himalayas, this larger-than-a-myna babbler is olive-brown above and ochraceous below. Prominent white throat bordered by an olive-brown band below. Terminal half of tail white. Forehead fulvous, a black mark in front of and below eye. A long rounded to graduated tail. Highly gregarious, keeping together in flocks even in the breeding season. Feeds on the ground, turning over leaves and twigs for insects, and on trees. A low, murmuring '*teh-teh*' call, turning to a noisy chorus when disturbed.

White-crested Laughing Thrush *Garrulax leucolophus* 28cm 1283

Tim Inskipp

Larger than a myna, this olive-brown bird of the forest undergrowth is found in flocks of around a dozen or more individuals. Prominent crest, head, throat and breast white. A black band extending from the beak, along the base of the eye, to well beyond it. Noisy and gregarious, feeding on insects, fallen fruit and such-like materials on the forest floor, turning leaves and fallen twigs, and keeping up a lively series of calls, bursting into 'laughter' now and then. The flock moves on in almost 'follow-my-leader' fashion, one individual after another flying and catching up with the others.

Streaked Laughing Thrush *Garrulax lineatus* 20cm   1314

Joanna Van Gruisen

A bulbul-sized laughing thrush, grey and chestnut in colour, with pale streaks. Ear coverts, wings and tail bright reddish-brown and characteristic of the species. Pale feather shafts prominent. Keeps together in small flocks, moving almost rat-like in the undergrowth. Usually keeps low down in the vegetation and going up only occasionally. Tends not to fly from tree to tree, preferring to get down into the undergrowth, crossing over and then clambering up once again. Has a variety of harsh squeaky calls, a '*chit-chit*' or '*chitrr-chitrr*' or '*pitt-wee-er*' and variants. Keeps to bush-covered slopes, open forest, coming rarely to gardens.

Brown-cheeked Fulvetta *Alcippe poioicephala* 15cm   1390

Krupakar Senani

Belonging to the genus of tit-babblers, this gregarious species behaves like both a babbler and a tit. It is a small, olive-brown babbler with a grey head and pale underparts. A species of the forest undergrowth found moving about in small flocks, rummaging through leaves and hanging on in all positions searching for insects amidst foliage and on twigs. Not averse, however, even to go on to the topmost branches of a tree. Maintains an almost conversational calling within the group. The song consists of four or five quavering whistling notes.

Tickell's Blue Flycatcher *Muscicapa tickelliae* 14cm　1442

Krupakar Senani

A beautiful, resident flycatcher with an attractive song. The male is a dark indigo-blue and rufous-orange bird, with the blue of the forehead, shoulder and eyebrow, brighter. The belly is white. The female is a duller version of the male. The throat is concolourous with the breast in both the sexes. A species of the forest, jungle, and wooded gardens, wary and not easily observed every time. Difficult to approach once disturbed. Seen usually in pairs in shaded areas, and has favourite perches. The call consists of a few repeated clicks, while the song is a nice little tune of over five notes repeated intermittently.

Verditer Flycatcher *Muscicapa thalassina* 15cm　1445

Toby Sinclair

A light sky- to bremen-blue flycatcher, breeding in the mountains of the north, and wintering all over the peninsula. The lores are dark and prominent, and the colour is brighter on the head and throat, darker on wings and tail. Eyes, bill and legs are dark. The female is duller, with the chin and sides of throat spotted with white, seen only under careful observation. Not easily sexed without the male around. A bold flycatcher of thinly wooded areas. Prefers exposed perches, flying to a different perch after every sally. Generally quite silent, but has a pleasing song.

Grey-headed Canary Flycatcher *Culicicapa ceylonensis* 9cm 1449

Toby Sinclair

A lively little flycatcher of wooded country. Rump and underparts bright yellow; head, neck, throat and breast ashy-grey, darker on crown. Back yellowish-green; wings and tail brown edged with yellow. A cheery bird which keeps to the shady under canopy or understorey of a forest, the Grey-headed Canary Flycatcher makes sallies after flying insects catching them with a loud snap, and tending to return to the same perch from which it took off. Also associates itself with the mixed-species, insectivorous bird flocks of the forest. The song is an enthusiastic and spirited trill, quite loud for such a small bird.

White-browed Fantail *Rhipidura aureola* 17cm 1451

E Hanumantha Rao

Belongs to a very distinct-looking group of flycatchers. A black, grey-brown and white flycatcher with a prominent fan-like tail. Sexes alike but the female is browner. Head and throat black; upperparts ashy-brown. The broad white bands extending back on either side of the forehead joining at the back to give a white nape. Lower plumage white. Tail brownish, all but the central feathers tipped and edged white, the white increasing progressively outward. A resident flycatcher found in groves of trees in open country and cultivation, in gardens and lightly wooded areas.

Asian Paradise Flycatcher *Terpsiphone paradisi* 20+50cm 1461

Krupakar Senani

One of the most distinct-looking flycatchers and hardly confusable with any other. Old males are pure white with head, crest and throat black, and the central pair of tail feathers elongated into extremely long ribbon-like streamers. Female has white replaced by rufous and no streamers in the tail. Very young males (1 year) are like the female, the tail lengthening with age, but the rufous remaining till around the third year. Found in shady tree-covered habitats. Has a harsh '*wich*' call, and a soft, warbling song rarely heard. Males never turn white in the Sri-Lankan subspecies.

Black-naped Monarch *Hypothymis azurea* 16cm 1465

S Nagaraj

A beautiful azure-blue flycatcher of woodland and forest, with a partial fan-like tail. Males have the upperparts deep azure-blue and the belly white. Head, neck, and breast brilliant lilac-blue with the black crest formed of short, erectile feathers. A crescent-like gorget on breast. Females and immatures have the head, neck and breast ashy-blue, the lower parts white and the rest of the body ashy-brown. A sharp interrogative '*wich*' or 'chwich' call, often given out in flight. Seen in the Himalayas, to about 1200m, east of Dehradun. Absent in arid north-west.

Zitting Cisticola *Cisticola juncidis* 10cm   1498

E Hanumantha Rao

A small warbler of grassland and cultivation, more often than not first spotted in its display flight. It is rufous-brown above, prominently streaked darker, unstreaked rufous-buff rump and white tips to fan tail. Sexes alike. The display flight of the male is a deeply undulating flight over its territory with a clicking '*zit-zit*' call given out at every undulation. Otherwise a typical warbler, secretive and skulking, gleaning insects in reed beds, paddy fields, other cultivated crops, and grass. Widespread, south of the Himalayan foothills. Absent in extreme north-west and Rajasthan.

Plain Prinia *Prinia subflava* 13cm   1511

Krupakar Senani

A typical wren warbler (or more appropriately longtail warbler), earthy-brown above and buff below, with an overall unstreaked plumage. The long tail is graduated and often held upright as in other wren warblers. A bird of tall grass and cultivation with a plaintive '*tee-tee-tee*' call; also an alarm call, and a song which is somewhat jingling and grasshopper-like. Shy and sulking, but certainly does not avoid man: often breeding in cultivation. Resident, but subject to some local movements, depending on local conditions and cropping.

Ashy Prinia *Prinia socialis* 13cm 1517

Vivek Sinha

 Smaller than a sparrow, this trim bird of gardens and scrub is a rich, ashy-grey above and buffy-rufous below; the shades varying between seasons. The chin and throat are white. The dark upperparts, which include the eye, are strongly demarcated from the underparts, giving it a trim appearance. The long, graduated tail is often held lifted. Moves about in the shrubbery and the like, hopping from twig to twig looking for insects, climbing up now and then to 'sun' itself in an exposed twig for a brief moment. Has a '*tee-tee-tee*' call-song given out from an exposed twig. The alarm call is a sharp '*kit-kit-kit*' and is not at all difficult to elicit.

Common Tailorbird *Orthotomus sutorius* 13cm 1535

Krupakar Senani

 Made more famous by its nest than by its looks, the smaller-than-sparrow Common Tailorbird builds its nest out of two or more living leaves, sewn together at the edges to form a nice little pouch for the eggs. A pretty bird to look at, the crown and head are rufous with green on the back and white below. A pair of black patches of skin on the throat visible when calling. The tail is long and pointed, held erect over the back, and has extended pin feathers in the breeding male. Generally found in shrubbery, but not loath to go up into a tree or come down on to the ground. Call-song not unmusical, a repetitive '*towit-towit*' or '*keea-keea*' sung from an exposed perch as in the Wren Warblers.

Paddyfield Warbler *Acrocephalus agricola* 13cm   1557

Sue Earle

A small, rufescent-brown winter visitor to the inundated reed beds and paddy fields. Throat whitish, with a pale supercilium. Smaller than a sparrow, with the tail rounded and the long undertail coverts extending to more than half the length of the tail. Active; found in low vegetation standing in water. Caution required in field identifying this difficult group. Distinguished from Blyth's Reed Warbler by a relatively more prominent supercilium, more rufous plumage, shorter beak and the wetter habitat. Has a characteristic *'chrr-chuck'* call. Breeds in north-west, parts of Western Punjab.

Lesser White-throat *Sylvia curruca* 12cm   1567

Joanna Van Gruisen

A migratory warbler of scrub and tree savanna, breeding over the greater part of Central Asia and Europe. Greyish-brown above and white below, with the white on the throat purer. Dark, almost blackish cheeks, ear coverts and eye patch give a masked appearance. Tail slightly rounded, not graduated and not long. Sexes alike. Quiet, unobtrusive, usually solitary and restless in habits. Skulks when disturbed. Has a habit of lunging out to seize an insect just out of reach, nearly toppling over in the attempt and quickly steadying itself on the wings. Found in open bush country, groves and gardens. A winter visitor, seen almost all over India.

Bluethroat *Luscinia svecica* 15cm

Nikhil Devasar

A bird of damp ground and heavy cover, the Bluethroat is migratory, unobtrusive and shy. The male is brown with blue throat and breast, and has the base of the outer tail rufous. A chestnut (occasionally white) spot in the centre of, and black and rufous bands below the blue. A prominent white supercilium, and buff belly. Plumage slightly variable. Female lacks blue, and has a blackish malar stripe which continues into a broken gorget of brown spots across breast. A great skulker, and extremely wary. Usually solitary, getting into cover with the tail almost doubled up on the back when disturbed. Has a '*churr*' or '*chuck*' call and an alarm note.

Oriental Magpie Robin *Copsychus saularis* 20cm   1661

Otto Pfister

A familiar bird of gardens, parks, woodlands and open forest. A pied black and white bird found hopping on the ground feeding on a variety of insects, perched on a twig, or calling. In the breeding season, the male mounts up to an exposed perch, usually on the outer side of a tree, to sing its rich, melodious song. Head and upperparts black, underparts white, with a white patch on the wing. Female similar, with the black replaced by a greyer shade. Takes to nest boxes easily. Usual call is a '*swee-ee*' raising at the end, and a harsh '*chr-r*' alarm call. Widespread, throughout the country up to about 1500m in outer Himalayas. Absent in extreme Western Rajasthan.

Krupakar Senani

A sparrow-sized migrant, frequenting rocky and stony areas with low-branching trees. The male has the head, breast and back black, the rump and belly being rufous. Central tail feathers brown. Crown grey in one of the races. Female has the black replaced by brown tinged with fulvous, and is paler below. A pale ring round the eye, with the belly also being duller. Beak and legs black inboth the sexes. A confiding bird in the winter quarters, perching on the low branches of trees quivering its tail, flying down to the ground to pick up an insect and flying back to its perch. Has a '*tictititic*' call, and a sort of a croak.

Plumbeous Redstart *Rhyacornis fuliginosus* 12cm 1679

Sue Earle

A small bird of torrential hill streams. But for the chestnut tail and the rufous lower belly, the adult male is all dull slaty. The female is grey-brown above, white and mottled slate below, with two rows of white spots on wing, and a pale eye-ring. The tail is white with a terminal brown triangle. Found individually or in pairs close to torrents and rushing streams in the wet zone of the Himalaya. Pursues insects over stones and boulders, or in the air, catching them in a short sally, even from the surface of the water. Very territorial. Has a '*kreee*' threat call and also a sharp '*ziet-ziet*' call. Crepuscular and active even well after dusk.

Brown Rock Chat *Cercomela fusca* 17cm

M S Oderoi

An endemic species to the subcontinent with a restricted distribution, the Brown Rock Chat is brown above, rufous-brown below, dark brown wings and darker tail. Looks like the female Indian Robin at first glance, but is larger and has no chestnut patch under tail. Found individually or in pairs; in rocky hills, ravines, ruins, old buildings, and bungalows. Can become quite trusting of humans, even boldly entering occupied buildings. A whistling '*chee*' and a harsh '*check-check*' call. A characteristic habit of bobbing the forepart of the body, partly spreading and raising the tail, and flexing its legs.

Common Stonechat *Saxicola torquata* 13cm

Foto Media/E Hanumantha Rao

A migratory species with a wide distribution, the Common Stonechat is a bird of the open country with rocks and scrub. Head and back black with white rump, wingpatch and collar. Has an orange-rufous breast paling towards the belly. Female is brown overall, streaked above and paler below, with a dark tail and white wing patch. Found individually or in pairs, perched on small bush tops, fence posts or boulders. A restless and wary bird, making sallies to pick insects from, but hardly ever moving about on, the ground. Alarm call a '*hweet-chat*' easily elicited. Breeds in Himalayas, 1500-3000m. Winters all over India except Kerala and parts of Tamil Nadu.

A familiar bird of open country, both cultivation and scrub. Male all-black, with white rump and vent (the extent varying between subspecies) and a prominent patch of white on the wing. The female is dark brown with rump and upper tail coverts pale rufous; the vent and undertail coverts pale reddish. Perches on top of a bush or such-like vantage point, looking out for insects on the ground, flying down now and then to pick them up. 'Spreads and jerks' its tail frequently. Has a trilling song and a harsh alarm call. Widespread, throughout the country, from outer Himalayas to about 1500m.

Grey Bushchat *Saxicola ferrea* 15cm

1705

A bird of scrub-covered and open hillsides. Male has a general pied appearance, dark ashy-grey mixed with black above. A white supercilium, a white patch on wing separating the dark wing quills from rest of the upperparts, and white underparts suffused with grey on breast and flanks. Sides of head, wings and tail black, the last margined with white, especially on the outer side. The female has the grey and black replaced with lighter and darker brown, with rusty upper-tail coverts and outer tail. Underparts lightly suffused with brown, darker on breast. A typical Bushchat in habits.

Tim Inskipp

A bird of rocky streams in the Himalayas and elsewhere, this species has a distinctive, pure white head cap, contrasting with the surrounding black plumage. Rump and underparts from the breast downwards are bright chestnut. Tail also chestnut, but with a black band terminally. Sexes alike; keeping singly or in pairs beside hill streams which are exposed and not covered by forest. Very territorial, catching insects carried by the current and those flying above in a quick sally. Has a shrill whistle. In winter descends to the Himalayan foothills.

Indian Robin *Saxicoloides fulicata* 16cm   1720

S Nagaraj

A common resident of rocky areas, scrub and open country, the Indian Robin is a bird which spends a lot of its time on the ground. Male overall black with a white wing patch and chestnut under the tail. The north Indian race has the upperparts brown. The female is brown, but without the white wing patch; undertail coverts chestnut. Hops about on the ground, with both the head and the tail held high! Feeds on insects, and likes termites. Tends to perch on rocks and stones rather than on shrubs and trees. Builds a small cup-type nest in a hole or a crevice in rocks and walls. May desert a nest on disturbance.

Blue Whistling Thrush *Myiophonus caeruleus* 33cm   1729

Krupakar Senani

Though not as fine a songstar as its southern counterpart, the Malabar Whistling Thrush, this species too has a whistling song which follows a fixed pattern with some variation, very human in quality but more clear and resonant. Pigeon-sized; overall dark purplish-blue spotted with brighter blue; forehead, shoulders, wing and tail also have brighter blue in them. Bill yellow and some white spots on wing. Sexes alike. In common with the group, has a loud and penetrating '*kreee*' alarm call. Found near torrential streams and gorges in heavy forest.

White-throated Dipper *Cinclus cinclus* 20cm   1773

Joanna Van Gruisen

As birds which dive into hill-stream torrents, Dippers form a unique group. Head, mantle, and underparts chocolate-brown; rest of upperparts slaty barred with brown. Pure white throat and breast. Has a close, thick plumage which effectively keeps away water when the bird dives amidst rocks, swimming underwater using its wings and even walking on the bottom. Tends to fly low over the water; feeds on aquatic insects and their larvae. Has a harsh '*dzchit-dzchit*' call. Found in rocky, icy torrents and glacial lakes.

Robin Accentor *Prunella rubeculoides* 17cm   1781

Joanna Van Gruisen

A bird of high altitudes, the Robin Accentor is pale brown above, streaked darker on the back, and has two whitish wing bars. Throat and head greyish with rufous breast. Belly is pale creamish. Sexes alike. A seed and insect eater, it comes into upland villages in winter; is usually gregarious around that time. Hops on the ground like a sparrow. Habitats found in are: Tibetan fades, damp ground, grass, scrub; and high altitude habitation. Breeds in high Himalayas, 3200-5300m. In winter descends to 2000m but rarely below 1500m.

Great Tit *Parus major* 13cm   1794

Krupakar Senani

A lively little bird of arboreal habitats, the Great Tit adds a lot of cheer around with its '*whee-chi-chi*' calls. A grey and white species with the head, neck and a broad, long band extending all along the ventral side being black. A prominent white patch on the cheek and a faint one on the nape. A typical tit, found in gardens, woodland, open forest, scrub with trees, parks and campuses. Searches foliage and the bark methodically for insect food, holding on to the twig in all acrobatic positions to get a better look. A hole-nester, visibly protesting at any nest intrusion.

Green-backed Tit *Parus monticolus* 13cm 1799

Toby Sinclair

A typical tit with white, greenish-yellow, slaty-blue and black in the plumage. Pattern of coloration quite similar to the Grey Tit: head and median band on the ventral side black, and a prominent white cheek patch. Rump, wings and tail slaty-blue, the latter two also have some black. A bird of a wide variety of forests, scrub with trees and such-like habitats, but generally preferring more moist conditions than the Grey Tit; a bird of the Himalayan hill stations. Calls lively and variable, not dissimilar to that of tits in general.

Chestnut-bellied Nuthatch *Sitta castanea* 12cm 1830

Krupakar Senani

A bluish-slate and chestnut bird which runs mouse-like on trunk and branches of trees, head up, head down, and occasionally even upside down on the underside of a branch. A prominent white cheek patch on the cheek and a black line extending from the line of the upper mandible to the nape. A very active bird, hunting for insects on the bark of trees, even in places seldom looked into by other species. Often a part of mixed hunting flocks or associated with other individuals of its own kind in small numbers. Found in deciduous and open forests, and other woodland habitats. Squeaky whistling and chirpy calls, and whistle-like song.

Yellow Wagtail *Motacilla flava beema* 17cm

R K Gaur

A typical migratory wagtail of moist meadows and water margins. Head pale bluish-grey with white chin, throat, supercilium and malar stripe; olive back and bright yellow belly. Brown wings and tail: the former with two yellow bars and the latter with white on the outside. Non-breeding and female's plumage duller. Found running about and picking up insects on lawns, grass, moist tank beds, drained paddy fields, and the like. Roosts communally. Flight typical of the family, deeply undulating, the birds travelling many tens of kilometres between feeding and roosting sites everyday.

Citrine Wagtail *Motacilla citreola* 17cm

1883

Nikhil Devasar

The region's only wagtail with a yellow head. Underparts, like head, a rich lemon-yellow. Wings and tail dark brown, the former having white edging to the covert feathers and the latter to the tail. Rest of upperparts grey or black depending on the race. A wagtail of wet, even squelchy, ground. Migratory, being found generally from September to April. Sociable and gregarious in its wintering grounds, keeping together with other species like White and Yellow Wagtails. Uses even floating vegetation in its quest for insects, and making an occasional short sally to catch a flying insect.

Grey Wagtail *Motacilla cinerea* 17cm 1884

E Hanumantha Rao

A sprightly migrant found in the greater part of the peninsula from September to April. Grey above, yellow below with whitish throat and breast; the extent of white being variable. Wings brownish with a yellow-white band. Rump yellowish; tail black with white outer-tail feathers. Usually found individually, running and feeding on the ground, making a brief sally to snap up a passing flying insect. Flight deeply undulating, with its 'chicheep' uttered in flight. Travels quite a long distance every day between its group roosting areas and its feeding zones, flying high above.

White Wagtail *Motacilla alba* 18cm 1885

Otto Pfister

A grey, black and white sparrow-sized migratory wagtail found singly or in groups. In winter, head black, back grey and underparts white. Sides of head white, the extent of white varying greatly between the various subspecies, and in the back being grey or black. Sociable, found in open country beside water: rivers, streams, ponds and tanks, inundated cultivation. Shares many habits with other wagtails like the deeply undulating flight, the vigorous moving of the tail and hindpart up and down when on the ground, walking and running, not hopping on the ground, and of course the active lifestyle.

White-browed Wagtail *Motacilla maderaspatensis* 21cm 1891

E Hanumantha Rao

The only resident wagtail of peninsular India. Much larger than other wagtails of the region. The plumage consists of just black and white, with black throat, breast and upperparts; white supercilium, wing band, outer tail and underparts. Sexes alike; female duller and browner. Colour pattern confusable with the Oriental Magpie Robin, but prominent white supercilium distinctive. Distinguished from other similar races of the White Wagtail by the forehead being black all the way till base of the beak. Prefers similar habitats to other wagtails, but also coming in to towns where they can be seen perched on rooftops.

Pale-billed Flowerpecker *Dicaeum erythrorhynchos* 8cm 1899

E Hanumantha Rao

A very active, diminutive bird drawing attention by its incessant '*click-click*' call and movement in the tree canopy. Olive-brown above and dull white below with no patterning. Bill pink, thinnish and sharp. Inseparably associated with mistletoe clumps on trees and large shrubs, irrespective of whether it is a garden or a jungle! The flowerpeckers as a group are the main dispersal agents for the semi-parasitic mistletoe family, *Loranthaceae*, feeding on their small fruits. Builds a small, hanging, pouch-like nest with a lateral entrance hole.

Purple-rumped Sunbird *Nectarinia zeylonica* 10cm   1907

A veritable gem in the sunshine, the male has five colours on it: upperparts metallic-green and deep chestnut, metallic purple rump and throat, the latter bounded by a deep chestnut band; rest of underparts lemon-yellow with the flanks off-white. Female is brown above pale yellowish below, with throat and breast ashy contrasting with rest of the underparts. The latter characteristic distinguishes it from the female Purple Sunbird. Very active, moving from twig to twig poking its beak into flowers to sip nectar, momentarily hovering in front of a flower to do so better; or perched on a twig twisting from side to side and singing away. Prefers moister areas than Purple Sunbird.

Loten's Sunbird *Nectarinia lotenia* 13cm   1911

The sunbird having the longest beak amongst all the ones that come into our parks and gardens; looks like a Purple Sunbird from a distance, but for the long beak. Overall metallic purplish-black displaying a green or lilac sheen with unglossed wing and belly. Iridescent, deep green throat graduating to metallic purple on breast followed by deep crimson-maroon band. Bright yellow armpits normally not visible with wings closed. Female olive above, yellow below with white tips to dark tail. Distribution restricted; avoiding dry areas. Generally keeps to tree canopy. A '*chewit-chewit-chewit*' song and a loud and sharp '*tchit*' call.

130

Purple Sunbird *Nectarinia asiatica* 10cm   1917

 Looking all-black from a distance or in bad light, the male is a glistening deep, metallic purple and deep blue. Female is olive-brown above and dull yellow below. Male in non-breeding plumage is more like female with a long, deep blue stripe running down the middle of the throat and belly. The female is distinguishable from similar-looking female Purple-rumped Sunbird by not having the throat ashy, thus making the throat concolourous with the rest of the underparts. Widespread, throughout the country, south from Himalayan foothills to about 1500m. Found in open forests, gardens and groves.

Oriental White-eye *Zosterops palpebrosa* 10cm   1933

 A small bird with a soft call, the Oriental White-eye forms small flocks which move from tree to tree in almost 'follow-the-leader' fashion. Olive-green above, and yellowish-green below; has a white ring round the eye, quite noticeable with a pair of binoculars. Essentially arboreal, feeding on flower nectar, insects and the soft pulp of fruits opened up by other animals, this bird also comes down to large shrubs when attracted by flower nectar. Has a song which starts inaudibly, grows louder and then fades away again. Builds cup nests in forks of twigs on trees. Found in forests, gardens, groves and secondary growth.

House Sparrow *Passer domesticus* 15cm   1938

S Nagaraj

So common and so widespread that it hardly needs a plumage description! Upper back chestnut, lower back and top of head ashy-grey; wings and tail brown, the former with a white bar. Underparts dirty white with the throat black, cheeks and sides of head pure white. Female dull brown with off-white underparts, reddish-white eyebrow and white wingbar. Gregarious, especially when roosting. Entirely commensal on man. Feeds on seeds, insects, and often omnivorous. Widespread, throughout the country, to about 4000m in the Himalayas.

Cinnamon Tree Sparrow *Passer rutilans* 15cm   1946

M S Oberoi

A sparrow of the hills, found near thin forests, human habitations and cultivation. Rufous-chestnut streaked with black on the back, a broad and a narrow white wing-bar, black chin and throat, greyish breast and flanks, and the rest of the body pale yellow, mark the male. The female is brown, streaked with dark brown above, and dull, ashy-yellow below, with conspicuous supercilium and wing-bars. A typical field sparrow, feeding on grain and seeds, forming large flocks which fly into trees when disturbed. Calls distinct from that of the House Sparrow, but similar.

Chestnut-shouldered Petronia *Petronia xanthocollis* 14cm 1949

Krupakar Senani

A tree sparrow of open country and cultivation, the Chestnut-shouldered Petronia is overall grey-brown, darker on the wings and the tail, much paler below, with a shallow, forked tail and a yellow throat. The shoulder patch is chestnut, while the wing-bars and belly are whitish. Sexes almost alike, with the female being much duller, including in the colour of the various patches. Not a house bird, this sparrow spends a lot of time on the trees; feeds on grain and seeds, insects and berries, and flower nectar. The calls somewhat resemble that of the House Sparrow.

Baya Weaver *Ploceus philippinus* 15cm   1957

Otto Pfister

The presence of this weaver in an area is literally proclaimed by the presence of the charact-eristic retort-shaped, woven grass nests. The breeding male has the crown and breast yellow; upperparts, throat and ear coverts darkbrown, and underparts cream-buff. The non-breeding male is similar to the female except for bolder streaks and paler supercilium: it is overall fulvous streaked darker anteriorly and dorsally, but is just darker on the sides of the head, breast and flanks. A bird of open cultivation with scattered trees. The nests are usually constructed at the tip of thin branches overhanging water.

Streaked Weaver *Ploceus manyar* 15cm   1962

S Nagaraj

Much like the common Baya Weaver in general habits and habitats, except that it prefers more wet conditions. Upperparts dark brown boldly streaked with fulvous, and underparts pale fulvous boldly streaked with dark brown. Yellow lines, one over the eye and one transverse, over the neck. In the breeding season the male acquires a bright golden-yellow crown. The nest of the Streaked Weaver differs from that of the Baya Weaver in not being pendulous but firmly anchored, and in having a much shorter entrance tube. Widespread, throughout the country, up to about 1000m in outer Himalayas.

Red Avadavat *Estrilda amandava* 10cm   1964

Krupakar Senani

A tiny bird of paddy fields and reed beds. Breeding male is white spotted crimson and brown, the latter on belly wings and tail. Head unspotted. Female is brown above and crimson on the uppertail coverts, spotted with white on wings and uppertail coverts. Lores black. Underparts saffron-yellow with the throat and breast more greyish. Non-breeding male is like female, but with the throat and breast more grey. Roosts communally. Every bit a munia in habits, but preferring wetter habitats than others.

Indian Silverbill *Lonchura malabarica* 10cm 1966

Joanna Van Gruisen

 A plain-looking, earthy-brown and white bird with a thick, conical beak. Main flight feathers black; tail rather long and graduated, and dark brown in colour. Upper-tail coverts white. Underparts pale buffy-white. Found in loose flocks, like other munias, even roosting gregariously. Prefers drier habitats than other munias, and is found in the neighbourhood of thorny scrub too. Feeds on small seeds like grain and millets, building a globular nest with a lateral entrance; more than one female laying in it and also being used as a dormitory.

White-rumped Munia *Lonchura striata* 10cm 1968

Krupakar Senani

 A blackish-brown and white munia of cultivation and lightly wooded country. A thick, conical beak and a pointed tail; with only the belly and rump white, rest of the plumage blackish-brown. A typical munia, gregarious when not breeding; feeding on seeds and insects. Roosts communally with other munia species in thickets. One of the munias which turns up and breeds even in deciduous forests, well away from any patch of cultivation. Has typical munia undulating flight.

135

Scaly-breasted Munia *Lonchura punctulata* 10cm   1974

Joanna Van Gruisen

A small and pretty, chocolate-brown bird of cultivation and parks. Chocolate-brown above with upper-tail coverts and tail yellow; white below with the abdomen banded with brown, giving a scaly appearance. Sites of head, chin and throat rich chestnut. Prefers more moist conditions than many other munias, being found in cultivation interspersed with bushes and scrub. One of the few munias which comes into city parks and gardens, even to build its nest there. General habits like other munias. Widespread, most of India. Absent in much of Punjab, north-western regions and western Rajasthan.

Black-headed Munia *Lonchura malacca* 10cm   1978

E Hanumantha Rao

One of the more colourful munias, the Black-headed Munia is essentially a bird of the marshlands. Head, throat and breast black, as are the undertail and lower belly. Back chestnut. Rest of underparts chestnut in the northern races, white in the southern race: essentially, the white of the underparts is replaced by chestnut in the north and the north-eastern races. Found in flooded areas like paddy and sugar cane fields, reed beds, and such-like habitats, even in forest clearings. Gregarious in the non-breeding season. Occurs in foothills and terai from South-east Punjab eastwards; most of north-east, Northern Orissa.

Collared Grosbeak *Mycerobas affinis* 22cm 1983

Foto Media/Joanna V Gruisen

A myna-sized, large finch commonly found on the tops of trees in coniferous and deciduous Himalayan forests. Male yellow, with head, throat, wings and tail black. Female has grey instead of black, and olive-green instead of yellow. The yellow thighs of the male and the absence of white wing patch in the female distinguish it from confusable species. The birds of this genus have massive beaks and feed on seeds of both conifers and broad-leaved trees and shrubs. They also take some animal food like insects, slugs and snails; and fruits and pine shoots.

European Goldfinch *Carduelis carduelis* 14cm 1989

Salim Javad

Only slightly smaller than a sparrow, with a crimson 'face', grey-brown upperparts and pale underparts, black wings and tail, the wing with a large yellow patch and the tail with white. Rump white. Tail and wing pattern distinctive in flight. Keeps together in pairs when breeding and in small groups otherwise. Feeds on seeds on or near ground, in orchards, bare hillsides, and open forest; going up beyond the tree line in the warmer seasons. Often sings in chorus in the breeding season. Breeds in the Himalayas, 2000–4000m. Descends to foothills in winter.

Yellow-breasted Greenfinch *Carduelis spinoides* 14cm 1990

R K Gaur

A small finch of cultivation, forest edge and hill station gardens in the Himalaya, this Greenfinch is found in pairs or small flocks. Brown predominates above and yellow below. Blackish-brown crown, ear coverts, malar streak, back, tail and wings; the last darker. Yellow underparts, rump, forehead, supercilium and sides of neck. Some white on the secondaries. Female is duller and more greenish. Ranges between 1100m and 4400m, extending upto the timberline on the slopes. Has a number of lively calls, twittering '*dwit-it-it*' notes; also a long-drawn '*weeee-chu-chu*', some even reminding one of the Iora's.

Common Rosefinch *Carpodacus erythrinus* 15cm 2011

Foto Media/R S Chundawat

A migratory, sparrow-sized finch breeding in central Eurasia and found almost all over the Indian region in the winter. Male has the crown and rump crimson, with the sides of the neck, nape and wings more brownish. Crimson throat gradually turns to whitish buff on vent. Female, like the House Sparrow, brown above, white below, with the anterior underparts streaked and two pale wing-bars. A typical finch, feeding on the ground and flying into trees when disturbed. Takes a variety of seeds and small fruit, and also flower nectar. Groups up with other species like buntings.

Rock Bunting *Emberiza cia* 15cm

R K Gaur

A bird of open conifer forests, and rocky country with grass and bush. Head bluish-grey, throat and breast bluish-ashy; rest of body chestnut-brown, streaked with black above, but tending to be more rufous towards the posterior. Outer tail feathers white, as are the supercilia. The cheeks are white too, enclosed by the 'ring' formed by black eye- and moustachial stripes. Two broad, black bands on the crown, each bordering the supercilium of that side. The female is duller. Keeps singly or in flocks, feeding on the ground and flying into trees. The tail is constantly flicked open, showing off the white.

Crested Bunting *Melophus lathami* 15cm

E Hanumantha Rao

The Crested Bunting is a sparrow-sized bird of rocky, stubble and fallow land. The male is all-black with the flight feathers of the wing and the greater coverts region chestnut. The prominent crest too is black. The female's crest is less prominent, and it is dark brown above and buff below: the feathers above are edged paler and those below are streaked and mottled with dark brown. Not as gregarious as the other buntings, keeping singly or in small numbers. Feeds on the ground on seeds and insects, and tends to perch on rocks or bushes. Roosts communally with other similar birds.

Index